WHSmith

Revision

Science

Mark Levesley

Age 11–14
Years 7–9
Key Stage 3

Hachette UK's policy is to use papers that are natural, renewable and recyclable products and made from wood grown in sustainable forests. The logging and manufacturing processes are expected to conform to the environmental regulations of the country of origin.

Orders: please contact Bookpoint Ltd, 130 Milton Park, Abingdon, Oxon OX14 4SB.
Telephone: (44) 01235 827720. Fax: (44) 01235 400454. Lines are open 9.00a.m.–5.00p.m., Monday to Saturday, with a 24-hour message answering service. Visit our website at www.hoddereducation.co.uk.

© Mark Levesley 2013
First published in 2007 exclusively for WHSmith by
Hodder Education
An Hachette UK Company
338 Euston Road
London NW1 3BH

This second edition first published in 2013 exclusively for WHSmith by Hodder Education.

Impression number   10 9 8 7 6 5
Year   2018 2017 2016 2015 2014

This edition has been updated, 2014, to reflect National Curriculum changes.

Cover illustration by Oxford Designers and Illustrators Ltd
All other illustrations by Fakenham Prepress Solutions, Fakenham, Norfolk NR21 8NN
Typeset in 10pt Helvetica Neue by Fakenham Prepress Solutions, Fakenham, Norfolk NR21 8NN
Printed in Spain

A catalogue record for this title is available from the British Library.

ISBN: 978 1444 189 339

Contents

Parents' guide

This book provides the very best available help for your child in tackling the demands of learning and revising the material in Key Stage 3 Science.

The book is a valuable resource to have at home to support your child's school science work throughout Key Stage 3. Each is also a fantastic revision guide, providing a clear and concise set of revision notes combined with strategies for maximising revision efficiency.

Active learning and revision strategies

Learning and revision are active processes! It's very easy to sit down and read something for half an hour and then think 'I've revised that'. However, we all know from experience how easy it is to realise 'I haven't a clue what I've been reading for the last 5 minutes'. To stop this happening, and to make the most of learning and revision time, this book continually challenges children with activities and questions, helping them to remain active in their thoughts. The book also teaches children a variety of revision strategies – proven ways that make it easier to remember things.

What can you do to help?

Revision can't be done by parents or guardians! However, you can help by taking an interest in your child's work, and some children will want you to test them. The Practice questions, with their answers, make this easy to do. As a challenge, ask one of the questions that appear at the start of each double page – these need longer, more detailed answers. All the information a child needs for their longer answers is in the units.

A bit of background

Key Stage 3 is from about age 11 to age 14 and is usually taught in Years 7–9. During this period of your child's education there are various compulsory subjects, of which science is one.

Units in this book

The material that your child needs to learn for science is set out in the National Curriculum. The order in which this material is studied is left up to individual schools. This book divides science up into biology, chemistry and physics, in common with most published courses and in line with the way in which science is most often taught in secondary schools. Each of these sections is then divided into series of units, each of which takes up 2 pages, making it easy to study from the book in small chunks. The units have been designed to match the most common ways of dividing up the material in schools, making it easy for you to match content from this book with the content that your child studies at school.

Features

- Practice questions on every page ensure that learning and revision is an active process, and this helps to make the science 'stick in the brain'!
- All questions have answers, so that children can learn from their mistakes.
- There are helpful aids to remembering things and these are highlighted in boxes.
- There are 'fact boxes' to add interest.
- There are questions at the start of each unit to introduce the main themes of the unit and to provide a check-list of what should be known after studying the unit.
- There is a full glossary, giving definitions of all the key scientific words used in Key Stage 3 Science.
- There is a full index and contents list, allowing you to find information quickly and easily.

Learner's guide

What is learning?

Learning is 'getting things to stick in your memory'. Sometimes this is easy and sometimes it's tricky. In this book you'll meet various ways to help you learn things.

The golden rule of learning is that 'it is an active process'. You actually have to concentrate and *do* something rather than just reading.

Use a separate file or exercise book to make your notes and diagrams, and to answer the questions.

Using each unit

Each unit starts with some questions in a green panel. These are the key questions that the unit will help you answer. See how much you already know by trying to answer the questions before you work through the unit.

Then try the 'Get started' question, outlined in blue. This is an open-ended question, but you can check your answer on pages 152–167.

Now read through and learn the information in the unit. The words in **bold** are important words you should know. Their meanings can be found in the glossary at the back of the book.

Finally, answer the numbered Practice questions and check your answers thoroughly.

Ways of remembering things

Throughout the book you'll find boxes like these:

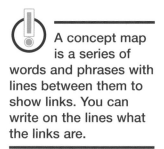

A concept map is a series of words and phrases with lines between them to show links. You can write on the lines what the links are.

FACT

About 8 million blood cells die in your body every second.

These boxes describe ways to help you remember things and give you interesting facts that help you to learn more about a topic. Try out the different ideas and you'll find that some work better for you than others. Once you've found the ways that work for you, use them for other things that you need to learn.

Here are some memory strategies to try:

Mnemonics

Pronounced '*nem-on-icks*', these are silly words or phrases that can help you remember the order of things in a list. For instance, the colours of the rainbow are red, orange, yellow, green, blue, indigo, violet. One mnemonic is a boy's name: ROY G BIV. Or you can use a silly sentence where the first letter of each word is the first letter of the word you need to remember: **R**ichard **O**f **Y**ork **G**ave **B**attle **I**n **V**ain.

Altered words

Misspell or mispronounce words on purpose to remember things (e.g. 'bears hi*bear*nate').

Links
Make up sentences where there are links between letters (e.g. *Bee* stings are treated with *Bicarbonate* of soda).

Saying out loud
Some people remember things better if they say them out loud. Doing this for all your revision might get a bit annoying (especially for those listening), so just try it with an important sentence or two – and try using a silly voice or doing an impression of someone.

Rhymes
Make up a silly rhyme (e.g. Righty Tighty – you turn taps to the right to tighten them).

Flow charts and drawings
Draw a silly picture...

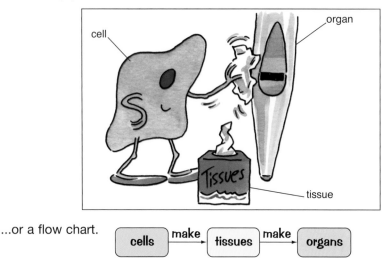

...or a flow chart.

cells —make→ tissues —make→ organs

Mental images
Create strange images in your mind. For instance, to remember that fish have scales think of a fish sitting on a set of scales.

Concept maps
Many people like to summarise their revision using concept maps. These take a bit of practice. They start with an important word or phrase in the middle and then other words and phrases are linked in, until you end up with a web showing all the links between many words and phrases. Adding drawings to a concept map really helps. Concept maps can be very large. Here's an example.

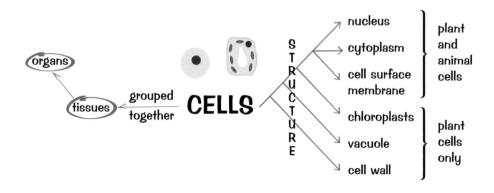

Repetition

Doing things over and over again is more likely to make them stick in your mind. It might be saying a sentence over and over, or doing any of the other things listed earlier. Repeating things is a very good way of memorising them.

Learning and your brain

The more recently a path through a forest has been used, the more obvious it is and the easier it is to follow. If the path is used often, it will be very easy to follow. If the path is lined with blue trees it will be even easier to follow! It's the same with memories. There are paths in your brain that lead to your memories. When you remember something you use a path. The things that you are most likely to remember are things that you learned recently, things that you repeated to yourself and learned again and again, and things that stick out. To get things to stick out use one of the ways of learning listed in the previous section!

A place in a forest is more likely to be found if there are more paths to it. If you learn a piece of information in different ways, you create different paths to that information. Use more than one way of learning each thing you need to remember.

Planning your revision

When it comes to revising:

- start early – well before an exam or test
- plan *what* you are going to do and *when* you are going to do it, and stick to the plan
- do a small amount at a time (say 20 minutes) and then have a break (say 5 minutes)
- don't have any distractions (TV, radio and iPods are generally not helpful)
- always *do* something as you revise (say things out loud, write things down, imagine things)
- you should aim to finish a revision session with some brief notes about what you have revised. Write these notes on cards. Later the same day look through the cards again to remind yourself of what you've learned. This is a really good, simple way of getting information to stick. And you can keep the cards to refer to again and again.

B2: Tissues and organs

In this unit you will learn to answer these questions:
- What do cells do?
- How are new cells made?
- How are sex cells used in plants?

Get started

Sperm cells swim towards egg cells. Neurones (nerve cells) carry information around your body. Ciliated epithelial cells have hairs called cilia that wave about to sweep things along. What cells are A, B and C below?

A   B   C

FACT

The longest neurone in an adult is about 1.3 metres long and carries information between the foot and the spine.

Cells have differences depending on their functions – cells are **adapted** to their functions. A neurone is long so that it can carry information a long way. Muscle cells can change length. A plant **root hair cell** has a bit sticking out of it that provides more area for water to get into the cell. These cells can quickly take water out of the ground.

Cells of the same type form a **tissue**. Lots of muscle cells form **muscle tissue**. Lots of root hair cells together are called **root hair tissue**.

root hairs

nucleus

Root hair tissue

When an **organism** (living thing) grows, its cells increase in number and get bigger. Cells increase in number by **cell division**.

Remember diagrams by drawing them from memory. Shut the book and draw cell division. Keep drawing it until you can get it all correct.

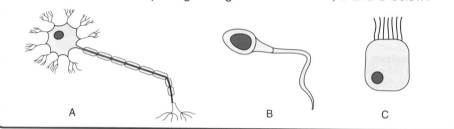

| parent cell | nucleus divides | new cell surface membrane forms | two daughter cells formed | daughter cells grow to full size |

Cell division

Practice

1. What is a tissue?

2. In which plant organ would you find root hair tissue?

3. How do organisms grow?

4. How are neurones adapted to their function?

Sex cells (also called gametes) are used to create new organisms using **sexual reproduction**. In plants the female gametes are **egg cells** and the male gametes are found inside **pollen grains**. These sex cells are created by tissues in the flower. The tissues are found in organs. An **organ** is a collection of tissues working together. The male organ (the **stamen**) produces pollen grains and the female organ (the **carpel**) produces egg cells.

The first stage of sexual reproduction in plants is when a pollen grain from one flower is carried to the **stigma** of another flower by insects or the wind. This is **pollination**. A pollen grain grows a **pollen tube** through the **style** and down to the **ovule** (which contains the egg cell). The nucleus from the male gamete in the pollen grain joins with the egg cell nucleus in a process called **fertilisation**, and a **fertilised egg cell** is formed. This will form the **embryo** of the **seed** and grow into a new plant.

The new nucleus formed in fertilisation contains all the instructions needed to make a new plant.

The stigmas of flowers contain sugar, which pollen grains need to grow a pollen tube. The amount of sugar affects how many pollen tubes will grow. In an experiment, six groups of 100 pollen grains were added to water containing different amounts of sugar. The bar chart shows the results of the experiment.

Lots of pollen grains were used in the experiment – a big **sample size**. If only a few pollen grains were used, it would be difficult to see the effect of the sugar since some pollen grains will never grow and one or two will always grow. Using a bigger sample size gives you stronger evidence.

> ! Draw a flow chart to show the stages in making a fertilised egg cell.

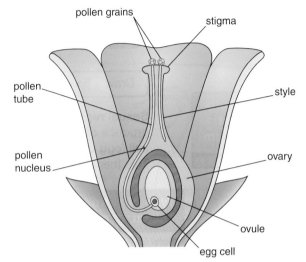

How a pollen grain nucleus reaches an egg cell in the female organ of a flower

> **FACT** Saffron is a yellow spice made from the dried stigmas of a crocus.

Practice

5 a In the experiment, what conditions allowed the most pollen tubes to grow?

b Write a title for the **bar chart** on the right.

c Why is it important to use a large sample size?

6 a Draw and label a root hair cell.

b How is it adapted to its function?

7 What tissue is this?

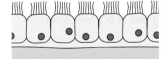

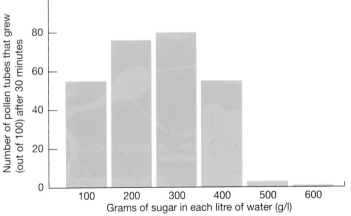

8 One cell becomes four cells. Draw a diagram to show how this happens.

B4: Growth and development

Get started

Once a fertilised egg cell is formed it turns into a ball of cells. Draw a diagram to show how this happens.

FACT
Fingerprints form about 8 weeks before birth.

Fertilisation occurs in an oviduct and the fertilised egg cell divides by cell division (see page 10) to form a ball of cells (an **embryo**). This reaches the uterus after about 3 days and **implants** into the lining. The embryo grows and a **placenta** and **amnion** form. When arms and legs are visible the embryo is called a **fetus** (pronounced '*fee-tus*').

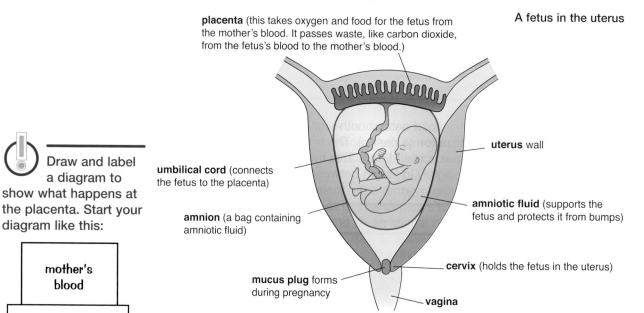

placenta (this takes oxygen and food for the fetus from the mother's blood. It passes waste, like carbon dioxide, from the fetus's blood to the mother's blood.)

A fetus in the uterus

uterus wall

umbilical cord (connects the fetus to the placenta)

amnion (a bag containing amniotic fluid)

amniotic fluid (supports the fetus and protects it from bumps)

cervix (holds the fetus in the uterus)

mucus plug forms during pregnancy

vagina

! Draw and label a diagram to show what happens at the placenta. Start your diagram like this:

mother's blood

oxygen

baby

Alcohol, chemicals in cigarette smoke and some viruses (e.g. rubella) pass through the placenta and can harm the baby or cause it to be born early (**premature**). Usually the baby is ready to be born after 9 months (the **gestation** period). The cervix gets wider and the uterus **contracts** (gets smaller), pushing the baby out head first. After the baby is born the placenta is pushed out (the **afterbirth**).

A new baby has no teeth and is fed milk to give it all the **nutrients** it needs to grow. Human breast milk contains **antibodies** that help to stop the baby getting diseases.

Practice

1 Why is a new baby given milk?

2 How is a baby pushed out of the mother?

A baby grows bigger as its cells divide. The baby grows into a child, then an adolescent and then an adult. **Adolescence** is the time when big emotional and physical changes occur in you. The physical changes occur during a period called **puberty**.

The changes at puberty are caused by **hormones** – chemicals that are made in your body and travel in your blood.

Draw out a time line from fertilised egg cell to adult. Label your time line with notes about what happens at each stage in the human life cycle.

The physical changes in males and females that occur during puberty

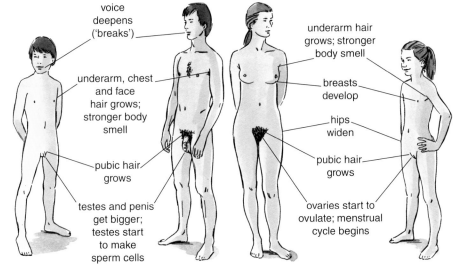

voice deepens ('breaks')

underarm, chest and face hair grows; stronger body smell

pubic hair grows

testes and penis get bigger; testes start to make sperm cells

underarm hair grows; stronger body smell

breasts develop

hips widen

pubic hair grows

ovaries start to ovulate; menstrual cycle begins

During puberty people grow much taller but different people enter puberty at different times. If you measured the height of every 12-year-old in the UK, you would find that, on average, girls who are 12 years and 6 months old are taller than those who are just 12. If you used a smaller **sample size** (e.g. girls in your school) you may not find this. Bigger sample sizes provide more reliable evidence.

FACT Robert Wadlow (1918–1940) was 2.72 m tall – the tallest person ever.

Practice

3 Write down a list of ways in which you have changed in the last 2 years.

4 Write another list of ways in which you will change in the next 2 years.

5 Oxygen gets into a mother in her lungs. Describe the route of oxygen from her lungs to her developing fetus's brain.

6 a What are hormones?

b What can they do?

7 Part of a letter in a newspaper reads: 'Both my children are taller than me, so I know that all children are taller than their parents'. Why is this piece of evidence not very reliable?

In this unit you will learn to answer these questions:

▶ How do cells use the food molecules absorbed after digestion?

▶ How does the oxygen needed for respiration reach the tissues of the body?

▶ What happens to the oxygen when it reaches the cells?

Get started

Which of these processes does the body need food for?

making new materials   providing energy   producing body heat

One of the small molecules produced by digestion is a sugar called **glucose**. This sugar is carried in your blood to all the cells of your body. In a cell, it is used to make other materials or to release energy in **aerobic respiration**.

In aerobic respiration glucose and oxygen are used up and energy is released (some as heat energy, which keeps us warm). The word equation is:

$$glucose + oxygen \longrightarrow carbon\ dioxide + water$$

All living things respire (use up food to release energy). Many require oxygen from the *air* to do this (*aerobic* respiration). The investigation shown below is designed to show that living things release heat energy as they respire:

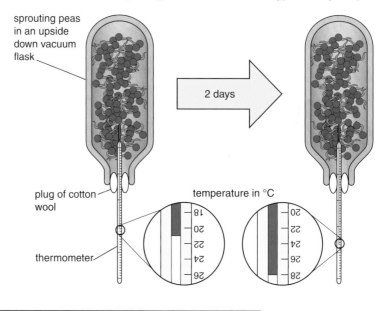

sprouting peas in an upside down vacuum flask

2 days

plug of cotton wool

temperature in °C

thermometer

Practice

1 a What is the temperature increase during the investigation with the peas?

b What does this show?

c What would happen if the peas were dead?

2 What are the reactants in aerobic respiration?

3 List the differences and similarities between aerobic respiration and burning.

Blood flows through an **organ system** called the **circulatory system**, which contains the **heart** and **blood vessels** (tubes through which blood flows). The heart is a double pump – it has two halves that pump your blood. The right-hand side of the heart pumps blood to the **lungs**, where it picks up oxygen from the air. The left-hand side pumps oxygenated blood to the rest of the body.

There are three types of blood vessels: **veins** carry blood to the heart, **arteries** carry blood away from the heart and **capillaries** are thin-walled tubes which carry blood through the **tissues** of the body. Oxygen and glucose leave and enter the blood in the capillaries and this is how oxygen and glucose are delivered to cells – they flow out of the capillaries into nearby cells. All cells need to respire to stay alive and so they all need a good blood supply.

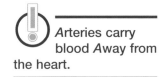

Arteries carry blood *Away* from the heart.

The carbon dioxide that is produced in aerobic respiration flows back into the capillaries and is taken by the blood to the lungs where it is breathed out of the body.

Sometimes your body can't get enough oxygen, such as when you run very fast. After a while you have to stop to 'catch your breath'.

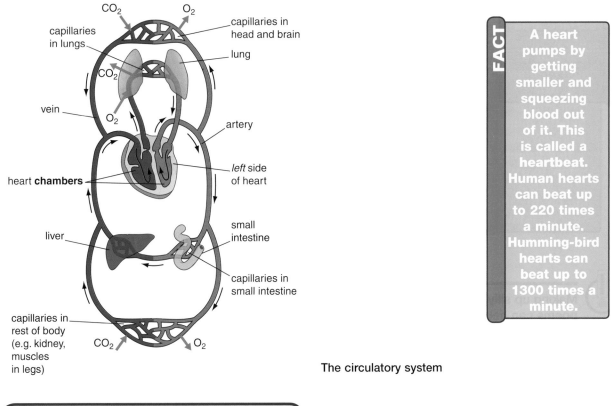

The circulatory system

Practice

4 What are the products of aerobic respiration?

5 Why is the heart called a 'double pump'?

6 Describe the route that a molecule of glucose takes from the small intestine to a leg muscle.

7 Describe the route that an oxygen molecule takes from the lungs to a leg muscle.

8 Why do all cells need a good blood supply?

B8: Microbes and disease

In this unit you will learn to answer these questions:
- What are micro-organisms and how do they grow?
- How can different types of micro-organisms be harmful?

Get started

Write down when you were last ill and how this illness was caused.

Microbes (or **micro-organisms**) are tiny living things that you need a microscope to see. Most are made of only one cell and are not plants or animals. There are three types: **bacteria**, **viruses** and some kinds of **fungi**.

The three types of microbes

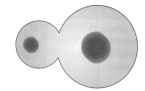

Bacteria often have 'tails' so they can swim.

Viruses are the smallest microbes – the largest viruses are only about 0.0000003 mm wide! They often look like spiky balls.

Some **fungi** are microbes – like yeasts. They are bigger than bacteria.

Some microbes are useful. For example, yeast is used to make bread dough rise. The dough rises due to carbon dioxide produced during aerobic respiration. An investigation was set up to see whether the amount of glucose in bread dough increased the amount that the dough rose by.

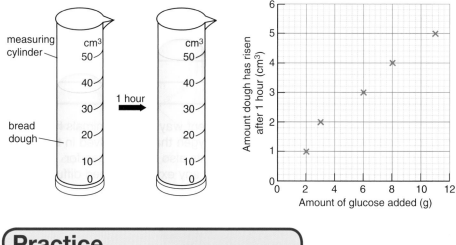

Practice

1
a What **factors** (**variables**) would you keep the same to make the investigation above a fair test?

b Why does the bread dough rise?

c What **trend** (pattern) can you see in the results?

d A **control** is part of an investigation where the factor being tested is left out. It is useful to compare the results of an investigation with a control. What would you *not* add to the bread dough in the control for this investigation?

e What would you expect to happen in the measuring cylinder during the control investigation?

Bacteria and fungi grow well if they are given a source of food and are kept in a warm place.

Growing bacteria and fungi is useful. Yeasts are used to make bread dough rise and to make alcoholic drinks (by **fermentation**). Bacteria are used to make cheese and yoghurt.

Growing bacteria colonies on an agar plate

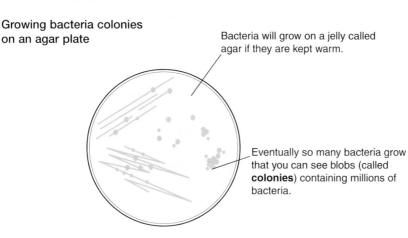

Bacteria will grow on a jelly called agar if they are kept warm.

Eventually so many bacteria grow that you can see blobs (called **colonies**) containing millions of bacteria.

Make three lists of bullet points, one list for each type of microbe.

FACT

Cows need bacteria in their guts to help them digest grass. The bacteria in one cow produce about 300 litres of methane a day – most is belched out and the rest is farted out.

However, some microbes cause diseases. These are spread from person to person in different ways.

Disease	Caused by...	Symptoms	Spread by...
AIDS	virus (called HIV)	certain cancers and becoming very ill from normally mild diseases	sex; sharing needles for injecting drugs
athlete's foot	fungus	red, itchy skin between toes	touch (touching an **infected** person or something that they have touched)
cholera	bacterium	diarrhoea, vomiting, muscle cramps	water (drinking water that has come into contact with sewage)
flu	virus	fever, sore throat, aches and pains	air (when you breathe in microbes that others have sneezed or coughed out)
food poisoning	bacterium	vomiting	food (eating foods like chicken that contain harmful bacteria that have not been killed by cooking)
impetigo	bacterium	blisters on the skin	touch

Practice

2 a List two uses of bacteria.

b Which of these temperatures would be best for making a food using bacteria?
   −10 °C   0 °C   10 °C   30 °C   100 °C

3 Design a poster for a doctor's surgery, giving people advice on how to avoid becoming ill with diseases caused by microbes.

4 Which of these is the odd one out and why?

   cholera   flu   food poisoning   impetigo

B10: Food and nutrition

In this unit you will learn to answer these questions:
▶ What's in food and why is it important?
▶ Which foods provide a balanced diet?

Get started

FACT

Without food you can survive for about a month. Without water you'd last 5 days.

Which of these sentences are true and which are false?

Carbohydrates are not found in food.

Fibre is found in meats.

Fats are used for energy.

Proteins are used for energy.

What you eat is called your **diet**. You need food for: energy, growth and repair, and health.

The food substances in a food are shown on **nutrition information** labels. You need different substances for different things.

Nutrition Information	Per 25g serving	Per 100g	
Energy	395 kJ (121 kcal)	1578 kJ (371 kcal)	When you want to compare foods always compare the same amount of each food (e.g. 100 g). Energy is measured in **joules (J)**. 1 **kilojoule (kJ)** = 1000 J. You need to eat food containing about 10 000 kJ each day. Kilocalories (kcal) is an old unit.
Protein	1.1 g	4.5 g	**Proteins** are used by your body for growth and repair.
Carbohydrate sugars starch	21.8 g 9.3 g 12.5 g	87 g 37 g 50 g	**Carbohydrates** are used by your body for energy. Carbohydrates that are not used up are turned to fat. **Sugars** and **starch** are different types of carbohydrate.
Fat	1.5 g	0.6 g	**Fats** are used by your body for energy. They are also stored in your body to be used for energy later. Stored fat helps to keep your body warm.
Fibre	0.5 g	2 g	**Fibre** is food that can't be digested. It helps to keep your gut healthy.
Calcium	113 mg	453 mg	**Calcium** and **iron** are examples of **minerals**. You only need tiny amounts of these to keep you healthy. Calcium is needed for healthy bones and iron is needed for healthy blood. 1 **milligram (mg)** = 0.001 **gram (g)**.
Iron	2 mg	7.9 mg	
Vitamin B6	0.4 mg	1.7 mg	**Vitamins** are also needed in tiny amounts to keep you healthy. Vitamin B6 is needed for healthy nerves.

Proteins, carbohydrates, fats, vitamins and minerals are all **raw materials** for making other substances in your body. Substances used as raw materials are called **nutrients**.

You also need fibre to keep your gut healthy, and lots of water. Water is used as a solvent, to fill up cells so they keep their shapes, and for sweating.

Add all the words in bold on this page to your concept map from page 17.

Practice

1 Draw a table to show the different nutrients in food and why they're needed.

2 a How much fibre is in 100 g of the food in the nutrition information label?

   b What is fibre needed for?

3 Write out a bulleted list of the reasons why you need to drink water.

We test foods to see what they contain. If you add brown **iodine solution** to a food containing starch, the colour changes to blue/black. If some dry food is rubbed on paper and held up to the light, a greasy mark is left by foods containing fats.

Different foods contain different nutrients. The food triangle below shows good sources of nutrients.

Food triangle

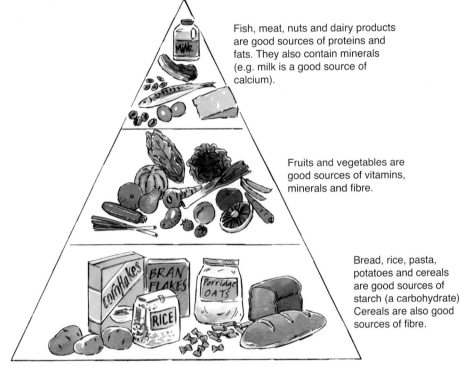

Fish, meat, nuts and dairy products are good sources of proteins and fats. They also contain minerals (e.g. milk is a good source of calcium).

Fruits and vegetables are good sources of vitamins, minerals and fibre.

Bread, rice, pasta, potatoes and cereals are good sources of starch (a carbohydrate) Cereals are also good sources of fibre.

 The mnemonic 'Enjoy GReat Health' reminds you what food is needed for (Energy, Growth, Repair, Health). Think up a mnemonic to remember the names of the nutrients.

You should eat a **balanced diet**. A balanced diet contains plenty of water, fibre and all the different nutrients in the right amounts. The food triangle above shows the right amounts – you should eat more of the foods in the lower part of the triangle. You should only eat sugary things once in a while.

Practice

4 a Name two types of carbohydrate.

   b Which carbohydrate should you eat lots of?

   c Which carbohydrate should you eat only a little of?

   d Name a good source of each type of carbohydrate.

5 a How would you test a potato to see if it contains starch?

   b What result would you expect?

6 Draw a table to show all the nutrients and fibre and two examples of a good source of each.

7 What nutrient should you eat the most of?

8 Design a poster for your kitchen fridge showing how to eat a balanced diet and why you need it.

FACT

Apart from the actual potato, the other parts of a potato plant are poisonous.

B11: Fitness – smoking and diet

In this unit you will learn to answer these questions:

- What do we mean by fit?
- What helps the breathing (respiratory) system to function?
- What is the effect of smoking on the lungs and other body systems?
- Why is diet important?

 Write three lists of organs found in the three organ systems mentioned on this page. Add a second column next to each list and write in it one important fact about each organ. Test yourself on your lists, covering up the names of the organs and saying their names using the facts, or the other way round.

Get started

Are you fit? Write down why you think you are or are not fit.

If you're fit then you're easily able to do all the things that you need to do each day. This includes things like running upstairs without getting out of breath. Different people have different levels of fitness.

The **organ systems** of fit people are usually working well, including the **breathing system** (or **respiratory system**) the **digestive system**, the **circulatory system**, the skeleton and joints. All these systems must work together to allow **aerobic respiration** to occur.

Practice

FACT

It takes about a minute for a red blood cell to go around the whole body.

1

a Make a list of all the organs you can see in the diagram below.

b Which letters on the drawing should these labels be matched with?

   i Lungs take oxygen from the air.

   ii The heart pumps blood around the body.

   iii Muscles take oxygen and glucose from the blood for aerobic respiration.

   iv The small intestine digests and absorbs food.

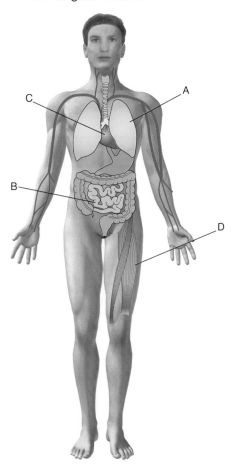

Smoking reduces your ability to be fit:

- **Tar** coats the **alveoli** surfaces in the lungs so less oxygen gets into the blood.

- Tar causes coughing, damaging alveoli and reducing their surface area.

- Tar causes cancer.

- **Carbon monoxide** stops red blood cells carrying oxygen.

- **Nicotine** is **addictive** and causes high **blood pressure** and **heart disease**.

- **Cilia** in the tubes of the respiratory system stop working and can't clean the lungs so smokers are more likely to get infections.

Smoke from cigarettes damages cilia in the lung tubes

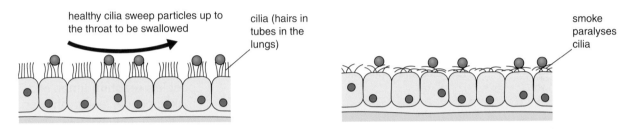

healthy cilia sweep particles up to the throat to be swallowed

cilia (hairs in tubes in the lungs)

smoke paralyses cilia

A **balanced diet** is also important to keep you fit and healthy. You need **proteins** to grow and to repair damaged **tissues**, **carbohydrates** for energy and **fats** to store energy and insulate your body. You also need water, **fibre** and small amounts of **minerals** and **vitamins**. The table shows some **deficiency diseases** caused by a lack of some **nutrients**. Eating too much causes **obesity**.

Nutrient lacking	Deficiency disease	Symptoms
protein	kwashiorkor	weak muscles and poor growth
vitamin C	scurvy	gums bleed and wounds don't heal properly
iron	anaemia	tiredness and shortness of breath

Draw a concept map to show how the different organ systems help you stay fit and healthy. You can add to it later. Start it like this:

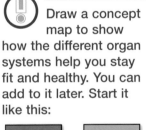

circulatory system

digestive system

fit and healthy

respiratory system — smoking
- tar
- nicotine
- chemicals in smoke

aerobic respiration

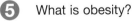

Practice

2 Why do you think fewer people smoke than they did 50 years ago?

3 Why do smokers:

a cough

b get more lung infections?

4 Why do you need to eat proteins?

5 What is obesity?

6 Find out the name of another deficiency disease and its symptoms.

B12: Fitness – drugs and exercise

In this unit you will learn to answer these questions:
- How does alcohol affect the body?
- What else can we do to maintain fitness?
- What effects do drugs have?

Get started

It is against the law to drive while under the influence of alcohol or drugs. Do you think this is a good law? Why?

A **drug** alters how your body works. Some drugs (**medicines**) are used to treat diseases; others are used for pleasure (**recreational drugs**). Many of these speed up the activity of your nerves (**stimulants**) or slow it down (**depressants**).

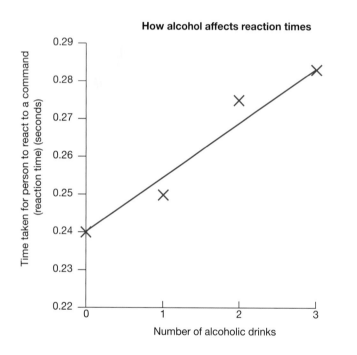

How alcohol affects reaction times

y-axis: Time taken for person to react to a command (reaction time) (seconds)

x-axis: Number of alcoholic drinks

Alcohol is a depressant. It slows people's **reaction times** and makes people feel uninhibited. In large amounts it can cause vomiting and even death. Too much alcohol over a long time damages the liver and brain, and stops important vitamins and minerals being absorbed from food.

Heart disease happens when heart cells die off. It is caused by a fatty substance blocking the blood vessels going to the heart muscle, reducing blood flow and starving the cells of oxygen and food. Heart disease is made worse by eating lots of fatty foods, smoking, too much alcohol and not taking enough exercise.

Practice

1. List two organs that alcohol can damage.

2. What is a reaction time?

3. What effect does alcohol have on reaction times?

4. Why are **alcoholics** at risk from deficiency diseases?

5. In heart disease, what don't heart muscle cells get enough of?

6. Think up four phrases to use on a poster about avoiding heart disease.

FACT In the UK about 9000 deaths are directly caused by alcohol each year.

Exercise helps to keep you healthy. It strengthens your muscles (including your heart muscles), strengthens your bones and improves your circulation.

If you over-exercise or do an unfamiliar sport too vigorously it can cause problems, some of which are shown in the diagram of the elbow **joint** and the shoulder joint.

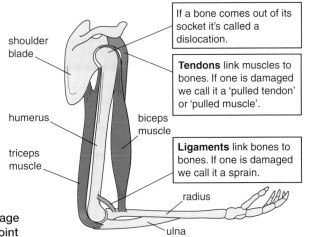

shoulder blade

If a bone comes out of its socket it's called a dislocation.

Tendons link muscles to bones. If one is damaged we call it a 'pulled tendon' or 'pulled muscle'.

humerus

biceps muscle

triceps muscle

Ligaments link bones to bones. If one is damaged we call it a sprain.

radius

ulna

Different types of damage that can happen to a joint

A joint is where bones are moved by muscles. Muscles can **contract** (get smaller and fatter) to pull on a bone, and then **relax** to stop pulling. However, muscles can *only* pull so a bone is moved by **antagonistic pairs** of muscles – one to pull it one way and the other to pull it the opposite way.

Some drugs can make muscles work better. These drugs are banned for athletes, so athletes have to be careful not to take medicines that may contain these drugs.

Recreational drugs are drugs taken for pleasure. Legal ones include **caffeine** (a stimulant), nicotine and alcohol. Illegal ones include cocaine (a stimulant), heroin and marijuana (both depressants).

Practice

7 a Name the two muscles that form an antagonistic pair in the upper arm.

b Why are antagonistic pairs needed to move bones at a joint?

8 What does a tendon do?

9 a What is a depressant?

b Give an example.

10 Write down some words that could be used to describe caffeine.

11 People think that we are healthier today than our great-grandparents were at the same age. Write down a question that you could answer by doing an investigation, to find out if this statement is true.

 Write out all the words in bold on pages 28–31. Go down your list and say what each word means. Use the glossary at the back of the book to check your answers. Write out the meanings of the ones you get wrong. Then go through your list again before going to bed tonight.

B13: Habitats

In this unit you will learn to answer these questions:

▶ How does the environment influence the animals and plants living in a habitat?

▶ How do environments vary?

▶ How do changes in a habitat affect the organisms living there?

Get started

Write a list of organisms that live underground. Can you identify one feature that all these organisms have?

Animals and plants have features that help them to live in certain areas. We say that they are **adapted** to where they live. **Adaptations** help organisms to survive. Here are some examples:

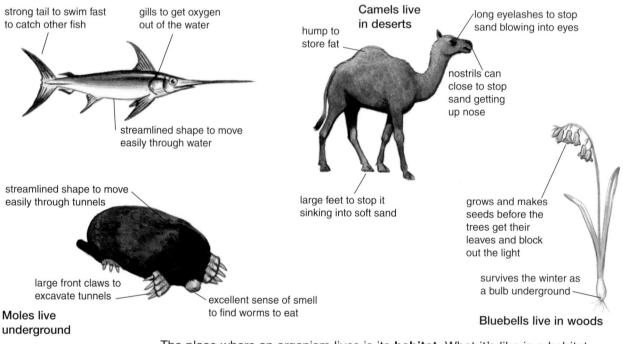

Swordfish live in an ocean habitat

strong tail to swim fast to catch other fish

gills to get oxygen out of the water

streamlined shape to move easily through water

Camels live in deserts

hump to store fat

long eyelashes to stop sand blowing into eyes

nostrils can close to stop sand getting up nose

large feet to stop it sinking into soft sand

grows and makes seeds before the trees get their leaves and block out the light

survives the winter as a bulb underground

Bluebells live in woods

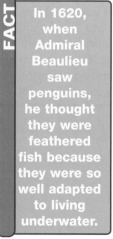

streamlined shape to move easily through tunnels

large front claws to excavate tunnels

excellent sense of smell to find worms to eat

Moles live underground

The place where an organism lives is its **habitat**. What it's like in a habitat is known as the **environment**. The environment of a habitat is caused by **physical environmental factors** (e.g. amount of light, temperature, wetness). Different organisms are found in different places in a habitat due to differences in environments.

FACT In 1620, when Admiral Beaulieu saw penguins, he thought they were feathered fish because they were so well adapted to living underwater.

Practice

1 Design and draw an animal that is adapted to live in the Arctic. Label your drawing.

2 Describe the environment in a desert habitat.

3 Many desert animals are the colour of sand. Why might this be a good adaptation?

4 Write a list of all the habitats mentioned on this page.

The environment in a habitat can change during a day. For example, it's light during the day and dark at night. These are **daily changes**. Organisms are adapted to daily changes.

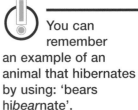
You can remember an example of an animal that hibernates by using: 'bears hi*bear*nate'.

Many owls sleep in the day and come out at night (they are **nocturnal**).

Sea anemones close up when the tide goes out so they don't dry out.

Ecologists are scientists who investigate habitats. They ask questions (for example: Where do dormice go when it gets dark? Do moss plants prefer dry or damp places?). Then they plan investigations, making sure that they only change one thing. So, if they are investigating how light affects woodlice, they keep everything the same (temperature, moisture, number of woodlice) and only change the amount of light. This is a **fair test**. They also make sure they use large sample sizes.

Habitats also change during the course of a year (for example, it is hot in summer and cold in winter). These are **seasonal changes**.

Hedgehogs eat a lot in the autumn and go to sleep (**hibernate**) in the winter when there is not much food around. Many plants stay below ground in winter (as bulbs) and trees lose their leaves because a lot of the water they need may be frozen.

Swallows leave the UK for the winter and go to South Africa where it is warm and there is plenty of food. This is called **migration**.

Arctic hares turn white in winter. This helps them to be camouflaged against the snow.

Practice

5 What is the difference between a daily change and a seasonal change?

6 a A deer grows thicker hair in winter. What sort of change is this?

b Why is this a useful adaptation?

7 Why do some animals hibernate?

8 Name one animal that migrates.

9 What is a fair test?

FACT Swallows fly about 16 000 km each year as they migrate. They can travel up to 300 km in a day.

B14: Feeding relationships

In this unit you will learn to answer these questions:
- What is a feeding relationship?
- What do food webs tell us?

Get started

Draw a diagram to show that foxes eat rabbits and that rabbits eat grass.

An animal that eats other animals is called a **predator**. The animals it eats are its **prey**. Predators have adaptations to allow them to catch and eat their prey. Examples include:

- forward-facing eyes for good three-dimensional (3D) vision
- sharp claws to grab with
- sharp teeth or beaks to rip flesh apart.

Prey animals have adaptations to help stop them being eaten. Examples include:

- excellent senses of sight, smell and hearing
- eyes on the sides of the head for all-round vision
- armour, horns or camouflage.

A **food chain** shows what eats what. The arrows show where energy goes. For example, in the food chain shown on the left, energy goes from the rose bush to the aphid because aphids eat rose bushes.

There are lots of other words you need to know:

- A **producer** is an organism that makes its own food (for example a plant).
- A **carnivore** eats other animals.
- A **herbivore** eats plants.
- A **consumer** eats other organisms.

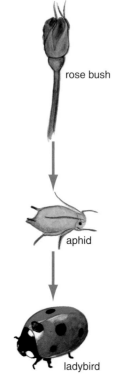

rose bush

aphid

ladybird

A food chain

Practice

1 What adaptations does a lion have for being a predator?

2 Write out the food chain shown above and write down whether each organism is a predator, carnivore, herbivore, etc.

FACT Cheetahs use speed to help them catch their prey. They can run at 70 mph.

Organisms in a habitat feed on each other. We say that there are **feeding relationships** in a habitat and we show these using a **food web**. A food web is lots of food chains all joined together.

The food web below is from a hedge habitat (even in a small habitat there are lots of different organisms).

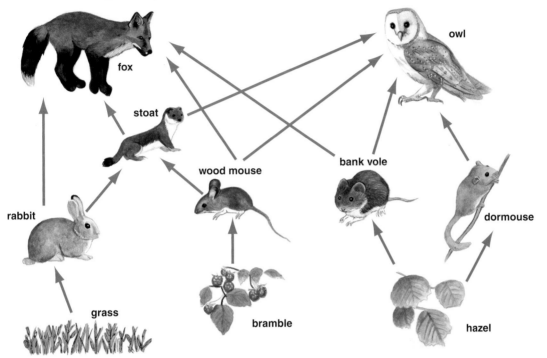

Scientists search for evidence in habitats to tell them what eats what. They watch animals, search for their tracks, and examine bite marks and droppings.

Many animals that are prey try to avoid being eaten! And some plants do too. Stinging nettles, for example, will sting animals on their noses.

The number of organisms of one type in a habitat is called a **population**. If you change the population of an organism it will affect the populations of other organisms in a food web. For instance, if all the brambles in a hedge are removed, the numbers of wood mice will go down because there's nothing for them to eat.

To think about changes in a food web, imagine that the arrows are pieces of string. Imagine tugging on the string connected to one organism and thinking about which other organisms will be able to feel this tugging.

Practice

3 Look at the food web above. Write down a food chain from the web with four organisms in it.

4 What do the arrows in a food web show?

5 What do owls eat?

6 Rose bushes are eaten by aphids. Hedgehogs eat earthworms and ladybirds (which like to eat aphids). Earthworms eat dead leaves. Draw a food web to show these feeding relationships.

7 a In the food web above, what would happen if all the hazel trees died?

b What would happen if there was a sudden increase in the number of rabbits?

8 Why don't rabbits eat stinging nettles?

B15: More relationships

In this unit you will learn to answer these questions:

▶ How do plants, animals and environmental conditions interact in a habitat?

▶ How big are the different populations in a habitat?

▶ How do living things in a community depend on each other?

Get started

How do foxes in a habitat depend on rabbits? What do rabbits depend on? Show this information as a diagram.

A habitat can contain many different environments – a pond is shallow at the edges and deep in the middle; a wood has shady parts and open clearings. Different organisms are adapted to live in different parts of a habitat so there won't be the same numbers of an organism in all parts of a habitat. The numbers of an organism in different parts of a habitat are its **distribution**.

Revision notes for the first paragraph might look like this:

habitat – different environments (e.g. pond depth) – different organisms

Try making notes like this from the second paragraph. Keep your notes and look at them again tonight and tomorrow to make sure they still make sense.

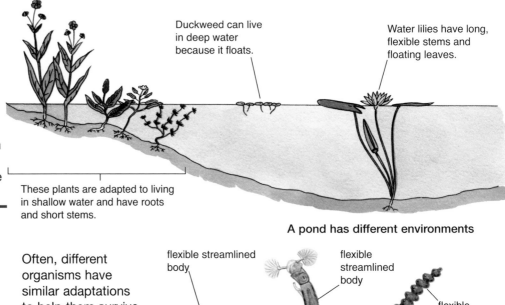

Duckweed can live in deep water because it floats.

Water lilies have long, flexible stems and floating leaves.

These plants are adapted to living in shallow water and have roots and short stems.

A pond has different environments

Often, different organisms have similar adaptations to help them survive in the same sorts of environment. For example, organisms that live in fast-flowing water have the same sort of adaptations.

flexible streamlined body

sucker to attach to rocks

flexible streamlined body

sucker to attach to rocks

flexible streamlined fronds (like leaves)

strong suckers (called holdfasts)

A hogsucker fish   **B** blackfly larva   **C** seaweed

These organisms are adapted to live in fast-flowing water

Practice

❶ Why don't plants with short stems live in the deep parts of ponds?

❷ What adaptations do organisms that live in fast-flowing water have?

❸ Which adaptation would be best for a plant that grows in shady areas?

big leaves   long roots   short roots   small leaves   thick stem

The populations of organisms in a habitat all affect one another. Trees, for example, create shade beneath them, preventing some plants growing there, but they also provide places to live and food for other organisms.

We use **food chains** and **food webs** to show what eats what in a habitat.

If the size of one population changes, it affects other populations. For example, if all the rabbits died some foxes might die from starvation.

Food chains show how the energy stored inside organisms passes from one organism to the next. At each step, some energy is used up (by moving, keeping warm) and some is lost in undigested food. Only some of the energy in an animal's food is stored in new materials inside the animal.

To survive, an animal needs to eat food containing a certain amount of energy. Since there is less energy as you go along a food chain, the populations of animals get smaller as you go along a food chain. The numbers of organisms in a food chain is shown in a **pyramid of numbers**.

sparrowhawk
thrush
fox
spider
rabbit
aphid
slug
grass
lettuce

A food web

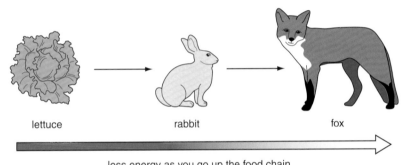

lettuce   rabbit   fox

less energy as you go up the food chain

A food chain

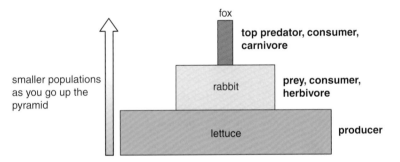

fox — top predator, consumer, carnivore

rabbit — prey, consumer, herbivore

lettuce — producer

smaller populations as you go up the pyramid

A pyramid of numbers

Practice

4 a Draw out the longest food chain starting with lettuce from the food web at the top of the page.

b Draw a pyramid of numbers for your food chain.

c What does a pyramid of numbers show?

d Why is a pyramid of numbers this shape?

5 The food web at the top of the page includes spiders. What would happen if all the spiders in the habitat died? Explain your answer.

In this unit you will learn to answer these questions:

▶ How can green plants be classified?

▶ How do plants, animals and environmental conditions interact in a habitat?

▶ How is a quadrat used to collect data to answer questions about a habitat?

Get started

FACT There are about 422 000 species of flowering plants alone.

Write bulleted lists of the things plants and animals need in a habitat. Try making other bulleted lists from the information on this page.

Make a list of the ways you could tell the difference between plants X and Y.

To survive, an animal needs water, oxygen, food and shelter. It also needs a mate to reproduce. Plants need light, water, carbon dioxide, mineral salts (nutrients), oxygen and space to grow. A **habitat** must provide these things.

X   Y

The conditions or **environment** of a habitat are caused by **physical environmental factors** (e.g. amount of light). An organism is **adapted** so that it can cope with the environment in a habitat. For instance, gills are an adaptation of fish that allow them to get oxygen out of their habitat – water.

Adaptations give different organisms different shapes and this helps us tell them apart. Animals are **classified** into groups like **vertebrates** and **invertebrates** (see page 50). Plants are also classified into groups.

plant kingdom

mosses
• reproduce using **spores** (tiny single cells)
• thin leaves without a **cuticle** (a waxy coating that stops leaves drying out)
• no roots or **xylem** vessels (tubes that carry water)

ferns
• reproduce using spores
• leaves have a cuticle
• have roots and xylem

conifers
• reproduce using **seeds** found in **cones**
• needle-shaped leaves with cuticles
• have roots and xylem

flowering plants
• reproduce using seeds found in **fruits**
• broad flat leaves with cuticles
• have roots and xylem

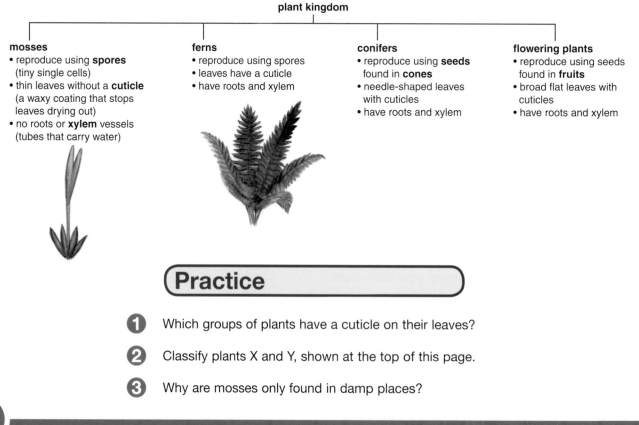

Practice

1 Which groups of plants have a cuticle on their leaves?

2 Classify plants X and Y, shown at the top of this page.

3 Why are mosses only found in damp places?

Ecologists are scientists who investigate habitats. They find out how many of each organism there is in a habitat. All the organisms in a habitat are known as the **community** and the total number of each kind is called a **population**.

Ecologists use equipment like light meters, thermometers and **dataloggers** to measure the physical environmental factors. They use **sampling** to find out what lives in a habitat and to **estimate** the populations. Taking samples means that they don't have to count every single organism!

A **quadrat** is used to estimate the number of plants in an area. The quadrat is thrown randomly 10 or 20 times and the number of plants of a certain type that are inside the square when it lands are counted. Knowing the number of plants in the area of all the quadrats thrown allows scientists to estimate the number of all the plants in the habitat.

- Sally counts 37 daisy plants in 10 quadrats.

- Each quadrat has an area of 1 m².

- So she has 37 daisy plants in 10 m².

- So there are 3.7 daisy plants per 1 m².

- The total area of the lawn is 190 m².

- The estimate of the number of daisy plants in the lawn is:

  number = 190 × 3.7 = 703

The more samples that are taken, the more sure you can be of the results (the more **reliable** your **data**). If you only take one sample, that sample may be unusual and give you a very poor estimate.

Using a quadrat to estimate plant populations

Practice

4 a Sameer uses a quadrat to sample a beach. He counts 54 sandwort plants in 10 quadrats. Each quadrat is 1 m². The beach has an area of 250 m². Estimate the number of sandwort plants on the beach.

   b Suggest an adaptation that sandwort plants might have.

5 Which of these organisms would you expect to find in a woodland community?

   cactus   fox   lion   oak tree   polar bear

   rabbit   seaweed   shark   snail   wood pigeon

6 Why are there different communities in different habitats?

B17: Photosynthesis

In this unit you will learn to answer these questions:
- How do plants grow?
- What is the role of the leaf in photosynthesis?

Get started

 Make sure you can write out the equation for photosynthesis from memory.

What do green plants need for photosynthesis? Unmuddle these words to find out.

LT HIG   ART WE   IRONIC DEAD BOX

The new material that an organism makes as it grows is called **biomass**. Plants make biomass using a chemical reaction called **photosynthesis**. In this reaction, water (from the ground) and carbon dioxide (from the air) join together to form a sugar called **glucose**.

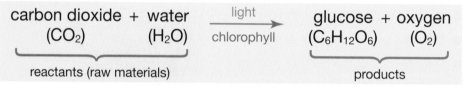

$$\text{carbon dioxide} + \text{water} \xrightarrow[\text{chlorophyll}]{\text{light}} \text{glucose} + \text{oxygen}$$
$$(CO_2) \qquad (H_2O) \qquad\qquad (C_6H_{12}O_6) \qquad (O_2)$$

reactants (raw materials)   products

To make this reaction happen, the plant uses a green chemical called **chlorophyll**. Chlorophyll absorbs light energy and uses this energy to make the reaction happen. Things that help reactions to happen are often written above or below the arrow in a word equation.

Practice

FACT Copper beech trees have brown leaves because another chemical hides the green chlorophyll.

The amount of carbon dioxide around an oak branch in a 24-hour period

Amount of CO$_2$ around one branch of an oak tree (y-axis)

0   2   4   6   8   10   12   14   16   18   20   22   24
noon

Time of day (hours)

1 Plants photosynthesise and respire causing carbon dioxide levels around their leaves to change.

    a Look at the graph above. What does it tell you about carbon dioxide levels around the oak tree branch?

    b Why is it this shape?

2 Why are leaves green?

Most of the glucose made in the leaves of a plant is then stored as **starch**. If leaves are boiled to remove chlorophyll and then iodine solution is added, the parts where starch is found will turn a blue-black colour. Starch is only found in areas where there was chlorophyll.

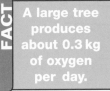
The other product of photosynthesis is oxygen and in *Elodea* pondweed you can see bubbles of oxygen forming. If more light is shone onto the pondweed, more bubbles are produced, telling us that photosynthesis is happening faster.

In land plants, oxygen **diffuses** out of the leaves through tiny holes called **stomata** (singular = stoma). Carbon dioxide diffuses into the leaves through the same holes. Most photosynthesis occurs in **palisade cells**, which are adapted to their job by being packed with chloroplasts containing chlorophyll.

Section through a plant leaf

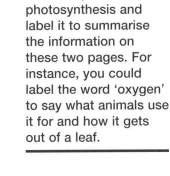

cuticle (waterproof coating)

epidermis cell

palisade cell

high O₂

low CO₂

spongy cell

low O₂

guard cell   **stoma**   high CO₂

Write out the equation for photosynthesis and label it to summarise the information on these two pages. For instance, you could label the word 'oxygen' to say what animals use it for and how it gets out of a leaf.

Animals use the oxygen produced by plants for aerobic respiration.

Practice

3 What is glucose turned into for storage in plants?

4 This is a variegated leaf, which only has cells containing chlorophyll in some areas.

a Which parts of the leaf would turn blue-black when tested with iodine?

b Why would these areas turn this colour?

c What part of a plant cell contains chlorophyll?

5 What happens to the speed of photosynthesis if a plant is given more light?

6 a What do animals need oxygen for?

b Write out the word equation for this process.

B18: More photosynthesis

In this unit you will learn to answer these questions:
- ▶ What happens to the glucose produced in leaves?
- ▶ What is the role of the root in photosynthesis?
- ▶ Why are green plants important in the environment?

Get started

Write a list of useful substances that we get from plants.

Some of the glucose made in photosynthesis is used for **aerobic respiration**, to provide energy for the cells:

$$\text{glucose} + \text{oxygen} \longrightarrow \text{carbon dioxide} + \text{water}$$

This process uses oxygen and gives off carbon dioxide. During the day, plants give off more oxygen than carbon dioxide but at night the reverse is true.

Every substance found in a plant is made using glucose as a starting point. This includes starch, cellulose (used in plant cell walls), fats and proteins. To make some substances, small amounts of **mineral salts** are needed from the soil. For example, mineral salts called **nitrates** are needed to make proteins.

Mineral salts, dissolved in water, are taken in by roots. Roots are adapted for absorbing lots of water quickly by being spread out and branched to cover a large area, and by having **root hair cells** to give them a large surface area.

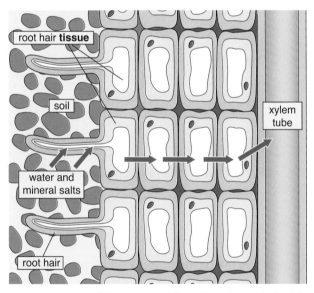

Structure and function of root hair cells

Practice

1. Why does an oak tree give off carbon dioxide at night?

2. Why will a plant not grow healthily if there are no nitrates in the soil?

3. Fertilisers contain nitrates. Why do farmers use fertilisers?

4. Sketch a root hair cell and label its parts.

5. How are roots adapted to their function?

Like all cells, root hair cells need oxygen to respire, which they get from gaps in the soil. If the soil gets **waterlogged** there is no oxygen in it and roots can die.

Once in a root, the water flows into **xylem tubes** (or xylem vessels) and is taken up the plant to where it is needed. Water is needed for photosynthesis, to keep a plant firm, to carry mineral salts, to fill up cells to allow them to grow, to cool down leaves and to form fruits.

Plants and other organisms that can photosynthesise (such as algae) maintain the balance of gases in the air. The graph shows that, over the last 600 million years, when the levels of carbon dioxide have gone down, the levels of oxygen have increased. This is partly caused by increasing photosynthesis. If we are to keep the current balance of gases (21% oxygen, 0.03% carbon dioxide) we need to ensure that there are enough plants to use up the extra carbon dioxide we produce in our vehicles and factories, and to produce oxygen.

A lot of the information on these two pages can be summarised as bullet point lists. Make up lists for the uses of water in a plant, the uses of glucose and the adaptations of roots.

Percentages of CO₂ and O₂ in the atmosphere over the last 600 million years

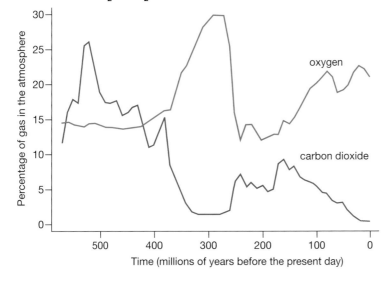

Percentage of gas in the atmosphere

oxygen

carbon dioxide

Time (millions of years before the present day)

Practice

6 A field gets flooded and the plants die. Why?

7 What is a xylem tube?

8 Why are plants important in maintaining the balance of gases in the atmosphere?

9 a Burning down trees in rainforests increases the amount of carbon dioxide in the atmosphere in two ways. What are these ways?

b State another problem caused by destroying rainforests.

10 Potassium is a mineral needed by plants. Find out why it's needed.

FACT Brazil produces about 300 million tonnes of carbon dioxide a year – two-thirds of this is caused by burning the Amazon rainforest. An area of forest about the size of Wales is destroyed every year.

B20: Growing plants

Get started

Write down some chemicals that a gardener might use on his/her garden and explain why those chemicals are used.

The amount of useful **biomass** that a plant produces is its **yield**. So, a wheat plant that produces more wheat seeds than another has a bigger yield. Things that reduce yields include not enough mineral salts, weeds growing near the plant and animals eating the plant.

Weeds are unwanted plants. Weeds **compete** with **crops** and take some of the things that the crops need (e.g. light, water, mineral salts), so there are less of these things for the crops, which grow less well and have lower yields.

Weeds are killed using **weedkillers** (**herbicides**). Some only kill certain plants – they are **selective herbicides**. However, killing weeds reduces the amount of food available for animals that eat the weeds. For instance, peacock butterfly caterpillars mainly eat stinging nettles.

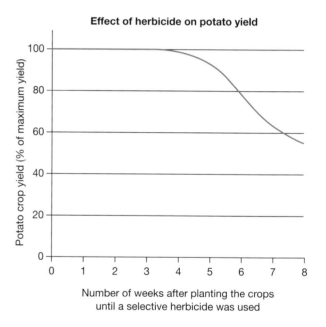

Effect of herbicide on potato yield

Potato crop yield (% of maximum yield) vs Number of weeks after planting the crops until a selective herbicide was used

FACT

Stinging nettle plants provide food and shelter for 107 different species of animal.

The numbers of weeds in an area can be **estimated** using a **sampling** method (e.g. using a **quadrat**).

Practice

1 What is a selective herbicide?

2 What does the graph above show?

3 Suggest three ways in which the yield of a crop could be increased.

4 A farmer destroys all the stinging nettles on a farm. State one effect this would have.

Pests are animals that damage crops. They compete with humans for food. Pests are often killed using **pesticides** but this means that animals that eat the pests have less food.

Pesticides and herbicides cause another problem when they get into food chains because they are not destroyed and remain **toxic** (poisonous).

Herbicide distribution in a food pyramid, showing bioaccumulation

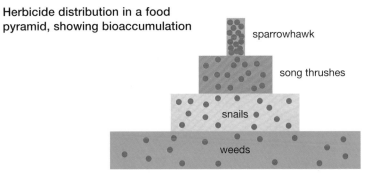

The pyramid of numbers above has red spots to represent a herbicide. As you go up the pyramid the same amount of herbicide is found in fewer and fewer animals, so each animal gets a bigger dose of the chemical. This is called **bioaccumulation**. It can kill animals at the tops of food chains.

Some crops are grown in greenhouses. These allow carefully regulated control of the temperature and the amounts of light, water and fertiliser that crops receive. This allows the crops to produce more yield and can also enable crops to be grown in places where they would not usually grow. However, greenhouses are expensive, can look ugly and plants grown in greenhouses sometimes don't taste like those grown outdoors.

Write the bold words on the last four pages on pieces of paper and their meanings on other pieces. Then match the words with their meanings. Keep your pieces of paper to revise from.

FACT There used to be 40 million vultures in India. There are now only a few thousand. This has been caused by a drug given to farm animals to relieve pain. The drug is poisonous to the vultures that eat dead animals.

Practice

5 What is a pest?

6 List the advantages and disadvantages of:

a using pesticides

b growing crops in a greenhouse.

7 Draw out the food chain shown by the pyramid of numbers above.

8 Here's another food chain: wheat → field mouse → barn owl

a Draw a pyramid of numbers for the food chain.

b Which is the pest?

c What problems might be caused by using a selective herbicide that only kills weeds in the wheat field?

B21: Variation

In this unit you will learn to answer these questions:

▶ How do individuals of the same species differ from each other?

▶ What are the causes of variation?

Get started

How are these two animals different from each other? List all the ways.

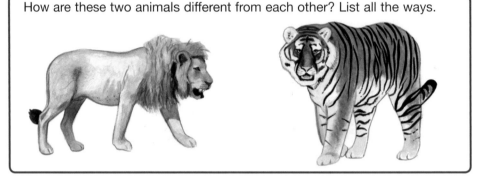

Organisms look different – we call this **variation**. There is variation between different **species** (for example lions and tigers) and there is variation between members of the same species (for example, humans all look different).

Scientists take measurements to compare one organism with another. You may have taken measurements like this at school (such as height, arm span, hand width, arm length). Scientists ask questions to investigate variation, such as: Are blond-haired people shorter than brown-haired people?

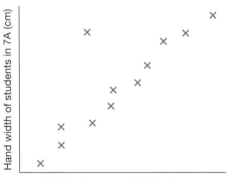

Scatter graph to compare hand width and height of students in 7A

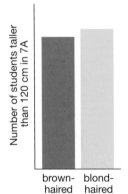

Bar chart to compare height and hair colour of students in 7A

The **data** are best displayed in a graph or a chart. You usually use a **line graph** or a **scatter graph** when *all* your measurements are numbers.

The scatter graph shows that, *generally*, taller people do have wider hands. We say that there is a strong **correlation**.

Practice

1 What is variation?

2 List three ways in which you are different to one of your teachers.

3 a What question do you think the scientists who drew the scatter graph asked?

b What correlation does the scatter graph show?

4 Does the bar chart show a correlation?

You will often find that children share similar **characteristics** with their parents. This is because some characteristics are **inherited** – they are passed from parents to children. In the family below you can see that Katie has inherited her dimpled chin from her dad.

Dad   Mum

Katie   Richard

Mum and Dad are not related to each other and so don't look alike, but Richard and Katie have inherited characteristics from each parent. The variation caused by inheriting characteristics is called **inherited variation**.

Inherited characteristics include things like eye colour, skin colour, a dimpled chin, lobed ears, hair colour and hair curliness.

Plants also have inherited characteristics, like leaf shape and flower colour.

However, our surroundings and what we do also affect our characteristics. Scars, sunburn and hair length are all examples of **environmental variation**. You also find environmental variation in plants (for instance height, colour of leaves).

Many characteristics are due to a mixture of inherited variation *and* environmental variation. Height is an example.

Writing lists with headings and subheadings is a good way of learning things. Write lists of characteristics caused by inherited variation, environmental variation and by both.

Practice

5 Who has Katie inherited her hair colour and type from?

6 A plant is not very tall. Write down as many reasons as you can think of why this might be.

7 Which is the odd one out and why?

sunburn   hair length   eye colour   scar

8 Draw a picture of yourself. Label all the examples of environmental variation down the left of your portrait. Label all the examples of inherited variation down the right.

B22: Classification

In this unit you will learn to answer these questions:

- How can we describe living things?
- How can we sort things into groups?
- How do scientists classify living things?

Get started

Write a list of similarities and differences between these two animals. What one characteristic is the best for telling these animals apart?

Scientists like to have names for organisms and to be able to tell them apart. The naming of organisms, based on what they look like and what they do, is called **classification**.

The drawing on the right shows a honey bee and the labels show the sorts of things that scientists look at when they are observing animals. All **insects** have three body parts and six legs, which is how you can tell them apart from **arachnids**, which have two body parts and eight legs.

Using their observations, scientists have divided all organisms into a number of large groups called **kingdoms**. The two biggest kingdoms are the plant kingdom and the animal kingdom.

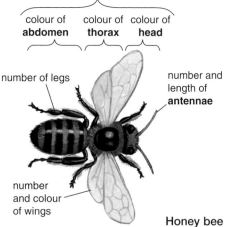

number of body sections

colour of **abdomen**   colour of **thorax**   colour of **head**

number of legs

number and length of **antennae**

number and colour of wings

Honey bee

Practice

1   a   The drawing on the right shows a bumble bee. How can you tell that it is an insect?

    b   How can you tell it apart from a honey bee?

2   What are kingdoms?

The animal kingdom can be divided into two groups – **vertebrates** (animals with backbones) and **invertebrates** (animals without backbones). These groups can then be divided into more groups. The diagram shows the characteristics of the different groups.

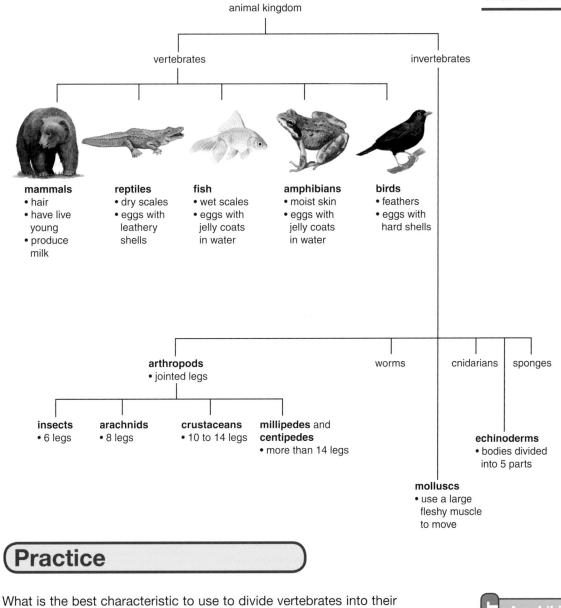

animal kingdom

vertebrates   invertebrates

mammals
• hair
• have live young
• produce milk

reptiles
• dry scales
• eggs with leathery shells

fish
• wet scales
• eggs with jelly coats in water

amphibians
• moist skin
• eggs with jelly coats in water

birds
• feathers
• eggs with hard shells

arthropods
• jointed legs

worms   cnidarians   sponges

insects
• 6 legs

arachnids
• 8 legs

crustaceans
• 10 to 14 legs

millipedes and **centipedes**
• more than 14 legs

echinoderms
• bodies divided into 5 parts

molluscs
• use a large fleshy muscle to move

Practice

3 What is the best characteristic to use to divide vertebrates into their different groups?

4 How are arthropods sorted into groups?

5 List all the groups that a bumble bee is in.

6 Make a large version of the diagram above using a word processing program on a computer. You could find some pictures of the different animals on the internet and add them to your diagram.

FACT Amphibians can take oxygen out of the air or water through their skin. They have lungs too.

B23: Inheritance

In this unit you will learn to answer these questions:

> What characteristics can be inherited?
> Why are offspring of the same parents similar but not identical?
> How do differences between offspring with the same parents compare with differences between offspring of different parents?
> How are new breeds of animal produced?

Get started

Charles   Mum

What kinds of **characteristics** has Charles **inherited** from his mum?

Sexual reproduction produces offspring that look similar to their parents but not identical. The differences in characteristics are called **variation**.

Cell nuclei contain **genetic information** stored in **genes**. **Sex cells** contain half the genetic information of a normal body cell. During **fertilisation** two sex cells combine and form a fertilised egg cell that contains a complete set of genetic information. Half of this is from the father and half is from the mother, so the offspring have characteristics from both parents.

Sex cells from the same parent contain slightly different genetic information. This is why brothers and sisters don't look identical.

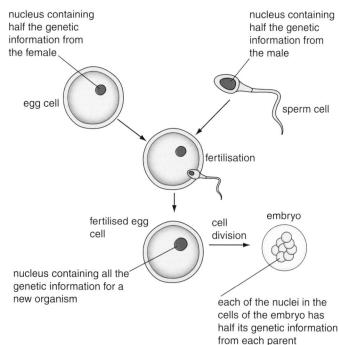

Fertilisation in humans

Practice

1. Sort these characteristics into those found in animals and those found in plants.

   blue eyes   brown hair   dimpled chin   lobed ear
   long roots   pink petals   small nose   spiky leaves

2. Think about a family you know. Write down two characteristics that a child in the family has inherited from his or her mother.

3. Why is the nucleus of a fertilised egg cell bigger than the nucleus of an unfertilised egg cell?

A **species** is a group of organisms that produce offspring that can also reproduce. Dogs and apple trees are both species. Within each species there is variation. A group of animals of the same species that share similar characteristics is called a **breed**. A group of plants like this is called a **variety**.

Some variations are easy to see (e.g. in apples – mass, colour) and others cannot be seen (e.g. softness, flavour).

The bar chart shows the results of an investigation. There is variation between the different varieties of apples and between apples of the same variety.

Differences in a variety are partly due to genes and partly due to **physical environmental factors**. For example, an apple on the sunnier side of a tree might be smaller, or apples on a tree that gets more water might be bigger.

German shepherd dogs and Border collies are different breeds of the same species

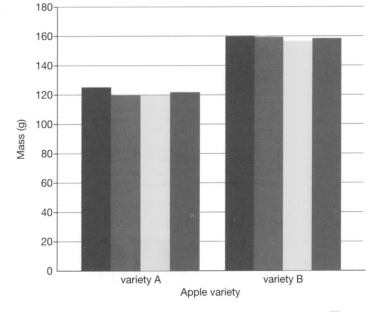

Comparing the masses of apples of two different varieties

variety A   variety B

Apple variety

Mass (g)

Practice

4 Look at the bar chart.

  a Which characteristic was being investigated?

  b Suggest another characteristic of apples that could be measured.

  c Complete this sentence to say what the evidence shows: 'Variation between the varieties is greater than...'

  d How could the measurements in the investigation be made more **accurate**?

  e How could the results from the investigation be made more reliable?

5 Is your height inherited or caused by your environment, or a bit of both? Explain your answer.

6 Identical twins have the same genetic information. What causes them to look slightly different?

 Draw a self-portrait and use it as a basis to add notes to summarise the information on these two pages. For instance, you could label inherited characteristics and characteristics caused by your environment.

In this unit you will learn to answer these questions:
- ▶ How are new breeds of animal produced?
- ▶ Why do farmers want new breeds of animals?
- ▶ How are new varieties of plant produced?
- ▶ Are varieties produced by selective breeding different from each other?

Get started

A fruit farmer wants to breed a new variety of strawberries.
What characteristics do you think these strawberries should have?

FACT

English lop rabbits have been selectively bred to have long ears. Some have ears over 75 cm long.

In **selective breeding** an animal with a useful inherited characteristic is bred from. The offspring that inherit the characteristic are 'selected' and used to breed from again. This process is repeated over and over. Eventually a new breed is produced (a set of animals that always have the characteristic).

For example, Border collie dogs are used to herd sheep. They were selectively bred to be able to follow instructions, and change speed and direction quickly. The table shows some other examples.

Animal	Characteristic that may be selected
pig	low-fat meat, quick growing
chicken	ability to live outdoors, lays lots of eggs, lays large eggs
cow	produces lots of milk, produces creamy milk

Sometimes a farmer or gardener may want characteristics from two breeds or varieties. **Cross-breeding** is when two breeds or varieties are bred together.

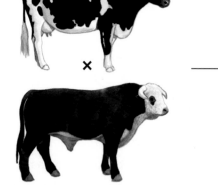

Friesian cows produce a lot of good quality milk.

Hereford cattle are good for meat.

Hereford-Friesian crosses are good for meat and milk. Notice that they also always have white faces – like the Herefords do.

Cross-breeding

Practice

1 Polly wants to breed very tall German shepherd dogs. What should she do?

2 Write down three characteristics that a farmer might selectively breed for in sheep.

3 What is cross-breeding?

Plants are also selectively bred. The table lists some characteristics that may be selectively bred. Not all of these characteristics are visible.

Plant	Characteristic that may be selected
apple trees	resistance to disease, lots of apples (a high **yield**), red apples, sweet apples
wheat	resistance to disease, lots of grain (a high yield), resistance to cold weather
tomatoes	deep red colour, sweet taste, tomatoes that last a long time without rotting

Pollen grains are normally carried from one plant to another by wind or insects. Plant breeders use paintbrushes to make sure that only the pollen from a plant with a useful characteristic gets onto the stigma of a flower. Once pollination is complete, the flower is covered with a plastic bag to make sure that no other pollen can get onto it.

When sex cells are made, they end up with only half the genetic information of a normal cell. Sometimes this half of the genetic information does not contain the information for the useful characteristic and so the offspring do not get the characteristic that is being selectively bred for.

Practice

4 What is a yield?

5 Look at the table above. Name two characteristics you can see and two that you can't when looking at the newly growing plants.

6 If you were to breed some pear trees, what characteristics might you selectively breed for?

7 Plant breeders cover flowers with plastic bags after pollination. Why?

8 Sinead wants to investigate whether the peas used for frozen peas are smaller than those grown to be sold as fresh peas.

   a What apparatus would she need?

   b How many peas should she use?

9 Ravi has cross-bred a thorny red rose and a thornless white rose in order to get a thornless red rose. However, he ended up with a thorny red rose. Explain why this might have happened.

Use all the words in bold on pages 52–55 to make a concept map. Start your concept map like the one shown below.

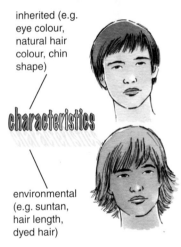

inherited (e.g. eye colour, natural hair colour, chin shape)

characteristics

environmental (e.g. suntan, hair length, dyed hair)

FACT

By cross-breeding pea plants, an Austrian monk (called Gregor Mendel (1823–1884)) discovered the basics of how characteristics are passed on from generation to generation. The science of genetics is based on his ideas.

C1: Acids and alkalis

In this unit you will learn to answer these questions:

▶ What are acids and alkalis like and where do we use them?

▶ How can acids and alkalis be identified and distinguished from each other?

▶ What is the pH scale?

Get started

Make two lists – what acids are like and what alkalis are like.

Acids are liquids that have a sour taste, although it is very dangerous to taste some acids! The drawings show some common acids.

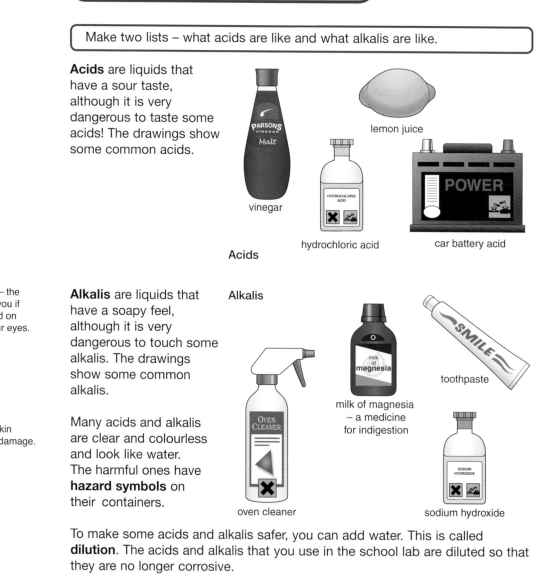

lemon juice

vinegar

hydrochloric acid

car battery acid

Acids

Hazard symbols

Harmful or **irritant** – the substance will hurt you if swallowed, splashed on your skin or into your eyes.

Corrosive – the substance attacks skin and causes severe damage.

Flammable – the substance catches fire easily.

Alkalis are liquids that have a soapy feel, although it is very dangerous to touch some alkalis. The drawings show some common alkalis.

Many acids and alkalis are clear and colourless and look like water. The harmful ones have **hazard symbols** on their containers.

Alkalis

oven cleaner

milk of magnesia – a medicine for indigestion

toothpaste

sodium hydroxide

To make some acids and alkalis safer, you can add water. This is called **dilution**. The acids and alkalis that you use in the school lab are diluted so that they are no longer corrosive.

Practice

1 Name two dangerous acids.

2 If you spill a strong acid you should add water to it before mopping it up. Why?

3 Design your own hazard symbol for poisonous substances. Check the answers to see how your answer compares with the real one.

Some parts of plants contain dyes that turn different colours in acids and alkalis. The dye from **litmus** moss is a purple colour. If acid is added to litmus it turns red. If an alkali is added it turns blue. Adding pure water doesn't change its colour.

Dyes that do this are called indicators. Other indicators include beetroot juice and red cabbage juice.

Some substances are neither acid nor alkali and so don't change the colour of an indicator. Substances like this are **neutral**. Pure water is neutral.

Lots of indicators mixed together make **universal indicator**, which has a range of colours to show how strong an acid or an alkali is. The strengths are measured on the **pH scale** – 0 is the strongest acid and 14 is the strongest alkali.

FACT
Hydrangea plants have blue flowers when grown in acidic soils and red flowers when grown in alkaline soils.

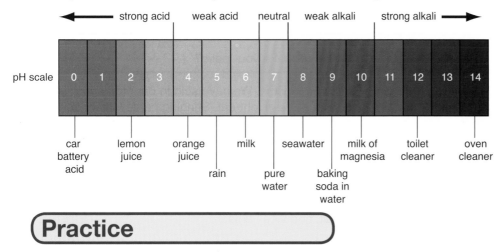

The colours of universal indicator and the pH scale

Practice

4 Vinegar has a pH between that of lemon juice and orange juice. What is the pH of vinegar?

5 Is orange juice a strong or a weak acid?

6 Name a strong alkali.

7 What is an indicator?

8 a What pH do neutral liquids have?

b Name one neutral liquid.

9 What colour does pure water turn:

a litmus

b universal indicator?

10 Make a copy of the pH scale above and find out the pHs of some more liquids to add to it.

C2: Neutralisation

In this unit you will learn to answer these questions:
- What happens when an acid is added to an alkali?
- Where is neutralisation important?

Get started

Sort these acids and alkalis into pairs of opposites.

| car battery acid | milk | milk of magnesia |
| orange juice | oven cleaner | seawater |

How did you decide on how to make your pairs?

Acids and alkalis are used by organisms. We have acid in our stomachs, which helps to kill harmful microbes that we might eat. Stinging nettles inject acids into the skin when touched. Many insect bites contain acids or alkalis.

Wasp stings are alkaline. We can make a wasp sting feel better by putting an acid on it, such as vinegar. Sometimes there's too much acid in your stomach (called indigestion or heartburn). **Antacid** tablets contain a weak alkali and are used to treat this. Soils that are too acidic to grow certain crops can be made less acidic by adding an alkali, and vice versa.

Inventing a silly sentence can help you to remember things. 'Bee stings are neutralised with Baking soda and Vasp stings are the opposite and are neutralised with Vinegar'. (All said in a silly accent!)

When an alkali is added to an acid, the pH of the acid rises towards pH 7. When an acid is added to an alkali, the pH of the alkali falls towards pH 7. Since pH 7 is neutral, we call this process **neutralisation**.

Practice

1. What is neutralisation?

2. How would you neutralise an acidic soil?

3. Why do antacids contain a weak alkali and not a strong one?

4. Are bee stings acidic or alkaline? How did you work out your answer?

A class wanted to find out which of four antacid tablets was best. They measured out 150 cm³ of hydrochloric acid (stomach acid) and added universal indicator. The acid had a pH of 2. Then they added powdered antacid until the pH was over 6. They repeated this with all four antacids and recorded the amount of antacid needed each time. The bar chart shows their results.

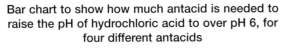

Bar chart to show how much antacid is needed to raise the pH of hydrochloric acid to over pH 6, for four different antacids

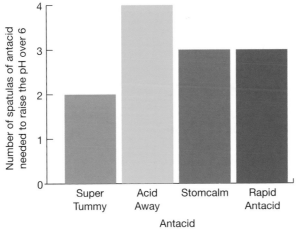

The class used a small spoon called a spatula to measure out the antacid. This was a fair test because they used the same type and amount of acid each time. The only thing they changed was the type of antacid.

Practice

5 Which was the best antacid? How do you know?

6 Write down a list of all the apparatus (equipment) that the group would have used for its investigation.

7 Think up some different questions about antacids that you could investigate. Think about how quickly they work or how much antacid different tablets contain.

A concept map is a series of words and phrases with lines between them to show links. You can write on the lines what the links are.

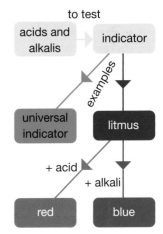

There's no right or wrong way to draw a concept map but it helps to make it colourful and to add little drawings. Try drawing a concept map using all the words in bold type on pages 56 to 59. Use the map shown here as a starting point.

C3: Solids, liquids and gases

In this unit you will learn to answer these questions:

> What are the differences between solids, liquids and gases?

> How are theories created?

Get started

Sort these substances into three groups: solids, liquids, gases.

air   carbon dioxide   hydrogen   milk   sand   stone   water   wood

There are three forms that a substance can take. It can be a **solid**, a **liquid** or a **gas**. These are the three **states of matter**.

Solids (for example a brick) have these properties:

- They don't flow easily.
- They keep their shapes.
- They keep their **volumes**.
- They cannot be squashed.

Liquids (for example orange juice) have these properties:

- They flow easily.
- They take up the shapes of their containers.
- They keep their volumes.
- They cannot be squashed.

Gases (for example air) have these properties:

You can really *feel* the air today!

- They flow easily.
- They take up the shapes of their containers.
- They expand to fill their containers.
- They can be squashed.

FACT

There's only one substance that exists naturally in all three states – water.

Do you find it easier to remember facts as lists with headings and bullet points or as a table? Draw out a table of the properties of solids, liquids and gases and find out!

Practice

1 Which states of matter:

a keep their volumes

b keep their shapes

c can be squashed?

Scientists try to explain why things are like they are. They ask questions like: 'Why can't liquids be squashed?' and 'Why don't solids flow?'.

Scientists make **observations** or do experiments to collect **data**. They then try to think up an idea (a **hypothesis**) to explain their observations and data. A good hypothesis can explain lots of things and can be used to say what will happen in future experiments – it can be used to make **predictions**.

A hypothesis that has successfully been used to make many predictions that have all been right is called a **theory**. Over time, theories can change and sometimes they are found not to be correct after all.

The theory that explains why the states of matter have their properties is called the **particle theory**. It says that everything is made of tiny little particles that you can't see.

Practice

2 What is a theory?

3 What is a prediction?

4 A certain substance can flow. What could it be?

5 What does the particle theory say that iron is made of?

6 Anil says, 'Water should be the only liquid.' If this were true, think up one way in which this would be a good thing and one way in which this would be a bad thing. Then find out an interesting fact about water.

C4: The particle theory

In this unit you will learn to answer these questions:

- ▶ How can the particle theory explain the differences between solids, liquids and gases?
- ▶ How can the particle theory explain dissolving, diffusion and gas pressure?

Get started

Imagine that you could look down a hugely powerful microscope and see particles. Draw what you think iron would look like.

There are two important points to remember about the particle theory:

- Particles are arranged differently in different states.

- Particles are always moving.

Particles in a solid are in a regular framework. They are held together by strong **bonds** and only jiggle about fixed positions. A solid cannot flow because the particles can't move past each other. A solid cannot be squashed because the particles can't get any closer to each other.

Particles in a solid

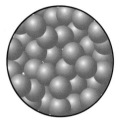

Particles in a liquid

Particles in a liquid are arranged randomly. They are held together by bonds that allow the particles to move past each other. This is why liquids flow. A liquid can't be squashed because the particles can't get any closer together.

Particles in a gas are not held together. They are whizzing around all over the place and that's why gases fill a container they're put into. A gas can be squashed because the particles can get closer together.

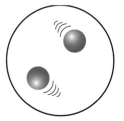

Particles in a gas

Practice

1 Draw diagrams of the particles in:

a magnesium

b helium

c mercury.

The particle theory can be used to explain **diffusion**, **dissolving** and the **pressure** of gases.

Diffusion is when particles spread through another liquid or gas. You can smell if someone is wearing perfume or aftershave because particles of the perfume spread through the air and reach your nose. The air does not need to be mixed for this to happen since gas particles are always whizzing around.

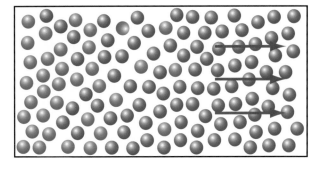

Particles of one gas (green) diffusing through another gas (blue)

If you drop instant-coffee granules into a glass of cold water, you will see a brown colour spread through the water. The coffee particles are diffusing through the water.

Eventually you can't see the coffee granules any longer because they have dissolved. Dissolving is when the particles of a solid have all separated from each other and spread throughout a liquid.

Gas particles hit the walls of the container they are in. The constant hitting of particles against the walls produces a pressure, which pushes out on the walls of the container. If you make the container smaller, but don't let any gas out, the particles hit the walls more often and the pressure increases.

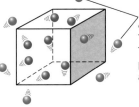

Particles of air hit the walls of the box from the outside. This is called air pressure. The pressure of the gas pushing out is matched by air pressure pushing in.

Gases produce a pressure on their container

Practice

2. You have been asked to write two definitions for a dictionary. Write down how you would define:

   a diffusion

   b dissolving.

3. A sugar lump disappears if it is dropped into hot water. Why?

4. If you suck all the air out of a tin, the tin crumples. Why?

5. Copy this diagram and add labels to explain how a drinking straw works.

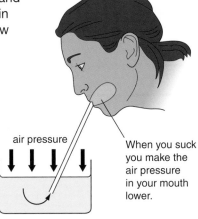

air pressure

When you suck you make the air pressure in your mouth lower.

C5: Atoms and elements

In this unit you will learn to answer these questions:
- ▶ What are elements made from?
- ▶ What are elements like?
- ▶ How are symbols used to show elements?

Get started

What do the materials in *italics* all have in common?

glass   *gold*   *hydrogen*   *iron*   *oxygen*   paper   rock   salt   sand

Everything is made of materials. There are so many different materials that it's impossible to count them all and new ones are being invented every day.

Materials are all made out of tiny particles called **atoms**. The drawing shows what a piece of iron might look like magnified more than a billion times.

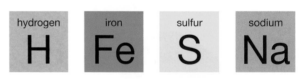

an iron atom

FACT

The smallest atoms are hydrogen atoms. One hydrogen atom is 0.000 000 05 mm across.

The atoms in iron are different to the atoms in gold. However, all the atoms in iron are exactly the same – they are all iron atoms. And all the atoms in gold are the same – they are all gold atoms. A material in which all the atoms are the same is called an **element**. Materials that contain lots of different sorts of atoms are **non-elements**.

There are 93 elements that occur naturally on Earth and all other materials are made from combinations of these elements. Each element has a name and a **chemical symbol** (one or two letters).

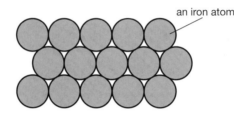

| hydrogen | iron | sulfur | sodium |
| H | Fe | S | Na |

Some elements and their symbols

Practice

1. Draw a diagram of what the atoms in gold might look like.

2. a What is the same about both iron and gold?

   b What is different about iron and gold?

3. Name three non-elements.

4. Sally says, 'All materials should be elements'. If this were true, think up one reason why this would be a good thing and one reason why this would be a bad thing. Then find out an interesting fact about elements.

Different elements have different **properties**. They can be divided into two main groups according to their properties – **metals** and **non-metals**.

Property	Metals	Non-metals
allowing heat to pass through them (**heat conductors**)	good heat conductors	poor heat conductors (except for diamond)
allowing electricity to pass through them (**electrical conductors**)	good electrical conductors	poor electrical conductors (except for graphite)
melting point	generally high – most are solids at room temperature	generally low
brittleness	are not brittle, can be stretched and will dent if hit	are brittle, cannot be stretched and fall apart if hit
examples	calcium, cobalt, sodium, nickel, potassium, iron	carbon, hydrogen, nitrogen, oxygen, sulfur, neon

All the elements can be shown in the **Periodic Table**.

The Periodic Table

Practice

5 Copy and complete these sentences:

The smallest part of any element is one _____.

A substance containing only one sort of atom is an _____.

6 Write a list of the properties of non-metals.

7 Where on the Periodic Table are non-metals found?

8 Pick five symbols from the Periodic Table and find out their names.

C6: Compounds and mixtures

In this unit you will learn to answer this question:
- ▶ What are compounds and mixtures?
- ▶ How can mixtures be separated?
- ▶ What are melting, freezing and boiling points?

Get started

Do you think that pure orange juice is pure? Explain your answer.

A **compound** contains two or more elements chemically joined together. If you heat iron and sulfur together you end up with a compound called iron sulfide, which always contains one iron atom for every one sulfur atom. If you simply mix iron powder and sulfur powder you have a **mixture** and not a compound.

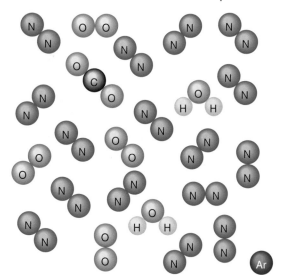

Air is a mixture of many different elements and compounds.

The numbers of the different atoms in a mixture can vary – you could add more sulfur powder.

A mixture, like air, is not **pure**. A pure substance contains only one substance – either a compound or an element but not a mixture. A mixture is always **impure**.

Mixtures can be separated. **Solutes** can be separated from a **solution** using evaporation or **chromatography** (see pages 69–71). A **solvent** can be seperated from a solution using **distillation**.

Air can be separated using **fractional distillation**. Air is first made into a liquid (at –200 °C). Each substance has a different **boiling point** and, as liquid air is warmed, substances with lower boiling points turn to gas before others. The gases are collected as they rise from the liquid air.

Gas in the air (only the main ones are listed)	Approximate percentage of air	Boiling point (°C)	Use
nitrogen	78	−196	filling crips packets so the crisps don't go soggy
oxygen	21	−183	breathing apparatus in hospitals
argon	1	−186	filling light bulbs

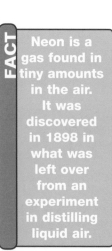
Practice

1 Why is air not pure?

2 Name a pure substance.

3 What other gases are there in air apart from those in the table?

4 Which gas boils and is collected first in the fractional distillation of air?

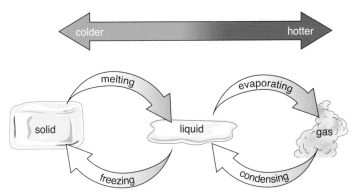

Practise writing out the diagram at the top of this page from memory. Keep doing it until you get it all correct. This is a good way of learning information from any diagram.

When a liquid is boiling, bubbles of gas appear in it. The temperature at which this happens is its **boiling point**. Fractional distillation relies on different liquids having different boiling points.

Some of a liquid is always changing to a gas (**evaporating**). At its boiling point a liquid can't get any hotter, and bubbles of gas are forming throughout its volume. Pure substances have definite boiling points. Mixtures boil over a range of temperatures.

A substance's **melting point** and its **freezing point** are the same temperature. For example, water at exactly 0 °C contains equal amounts of liquid and ice. Very slightly above 0 °C it will all be liquid, and very slightly below it will all be solid. Pure substances have definite melting and freezing points. Impure substances melt and freeze over a range of temperatures.

To see if something is pure you can test it to see if it has an exact boiling point, or an exact melting or freezing point.

FACT

Putting salt on the roads in winter causes ice to melt because salty water has a lower melting point than pure water.

Practice

5 Which phrase best completes this sentence: 'Boiling point is the temperature at which...'

A ...a liquid turns to a gas.

B ...a gas turns into a liquid.

C ...a liquid is as hot as it can get.

6 Look at the table on the facing page.

a What temperature does nitrogen boil at?

b What range of temperatures does air boil at?

c You have a liquid at –200 °C. How could you find out if it was pure nitrogen?

7 The melting point of gold is 1064 °C. What is its freezing point?

8 Would you expect frozen orange juice to have a definite, exact melting point? Explain your answer.

C7: Solutions

In this unit you will learn to answer these questions:

▶ How can we tell whether a liquid is a mixture?

▶ What happens to the solute when a solution is made?

▶ How can we separate solvents from solutes?

Get started

Which is the odd one out and why?

brick   cement   salt   sand   steel   stone

When a substance **dissolves** we often can't see it any longer, but it's still there; it's just that its particles have separated and spread out. Solids that dissolve are said to be **soluble**. Solids that don't dissolve are **insoluble**.

Seawater contains salt dissolved in water. It is a **mixture** of more than one substance. You can't see the salt in seawater, but you know it's there because it tastes salty. If you let some seawater dry out, the water turns to gas and leaves behind the salt.

Rock salt is a mixture of salt and rock. To make pure salt you stir crushed rock salt with water. The salt dissolves but the rock doesn't. You then **filter** the mixture to remove the insoluble rock, and then evaporate the water to leave behind the salt.

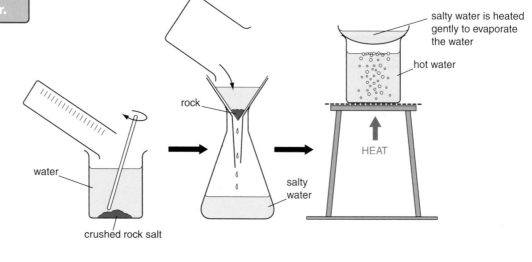

Getting pure salt from rock salt

Practice

1 What is a mixture?

2 Which of these are soluble?

plastic   salt   sand   stone   sugar   wood

3 Some rock salt had a mass of 100 g. The salt obtained from it had a mass of 40 g. Why did the salt have less mass than the rock salt?

When you dissolve a solid in a liquid you get a **solution**. A solution is always see-through. If you mix an insoluble solid in a liquid you often get a **suspension** (e.g. muddy water). Suspensions are not see-through.

Salty water is a solution of salt and water. The substance that has dissolved is the **solute** and the liquid is the **solvent**. The mass of a solution is the same as the mass of the solvent plus the mass of the solute. No matter is lost during dissolving.

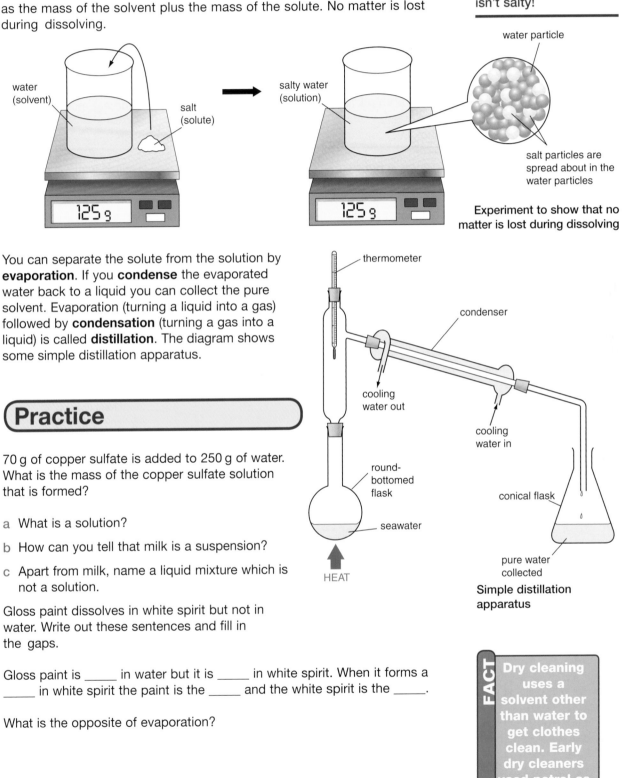

water (solvent)

salt (solute)

salty water (solution)

water particle

salt particles are spread about in the water particles

Experiment to show that no matter is lost during dissolving

Remember that only sol**V**ents e**V**aporate. Solutes don't and they get left behind. That's why rain isn't salty!

You can separate the solute from the solution by **evaporation**. If you **condense** the evaporated water back to a liquid you can collect the pure solvent. Evaporation (turning a liquid into a gas) followed by **condensation** (turning a gas into a liquid) is called **distillation**. The diagram shows some simple distillation apparatus.

thermometer

condenser

cooling water out

cooling water in

round-bottomed flask

conical flask

seawater

HEAT

pure water collected

Simple distillation apparatus

Practice

4. 70 g of copper sulfate is added to 250 g of water. What is the mass of the copper sulfate solution that is formed?

5. a What is a solution?

   b How can you tell that milk is a suspension?

   c Apart from milk, name a liquid mixture which is not a solution.

6. Gloss paint dissolves in white spirit but not in water. Write out these sentences and fill in the gaps.

   Gloss paint is _____ in water but it is _____ in white spirit. When it forms a _____ in white spirit the paint is the _____ and the white spirit is the _____.

7. What is the opposite of evaporation?

FACT

Dry cleaning uses a solvent other than water to get clothes clean. Early dry cleaners used petrol as the solvent!

C8: More about dissolving

In this unit you will learn to answer these questions:

- How can chromatography separate and identify substances in mixtures?
- Is there a limit to the amount of solid that will dissolve in a liquid?

Get started

Which of these liquids are one pure substance and which are mixtures?

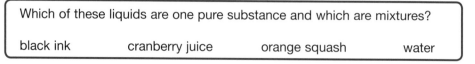

black ink   cranberry juice   orange squash   water

In science, a **pure** substance contains only one thing. Distilled water is pure but tap water, seawater and mineral water are mixtures; they are not pure water.

If a solution contains different solutes you can often separate them using **chromatography**. The diagram shows a **chromatogram** made by doing chromatography on four different inks.

 Labelled diagrams are a good way to learn things. Draw a labelled diagram to summarise the information on this page.

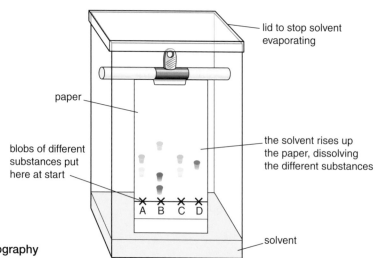

lid to stop solvent evaporating

paper

blobs of different substances put here at start

the solvent rises up the paper, dissolving the different substances

A B C D

solvent

Chromatography

Different solutes have different particle sizes. Larger particles travel more slowly than smaller ones and so the solutes are separated. Blobs of the same colour that reach the same height on the chromatogram are the same substance.

Solutes in urine are separated using chromatography in hospitals. Stains are used to make the solutes show up.

FACT The Food Standards Agency uses chromatography to check that foods don't contain things that they shouldn't.

Practice

1 What is a pure substance?

2 Look at the chromatogram.
a Is ink B a pure substance?
b How do you know?
c Which ink contains only one dye?
d Which two inks are the same?

3 Why would a hospital want to find out what was in someone's urine?

When you add sugar to hot tea it dissolves, but there is a maximum amount of sugar you can add. When no more of a solute will dissolve in a solvent you have a **saturated solution**.

The amount of a solute that will dissolve in a certain amount of solvent is its **solubility**. The table on the right shows how much of various solutes will dissolve in 100 cm³ of water at 25 °C. Different solutes have different solubilities.

Generally, you can increase a substance's solubility by increasing the temperature. The graph shows how the solubility of sugar increases with temperature.

Substance	Solubility at 25°C (g/100 cm³ of water)
aspirin	0.33
sodium hydroxide	42
sugar	211
salt (sodium chloride)	35.7

Practice

4 a What is a saturated solution?

  b How could you make a saturated solution of sugar in water?

5 Look at the table above. Which substance is:

  a the most soluble

  b the least soluble?

6 Look at the graph.

  a What happens to the solubility of sugar as the temperature increases?

  b What is the solubility of sugar at 0 °C?

  c What do you think the solubility of salt will be at 100 °C?

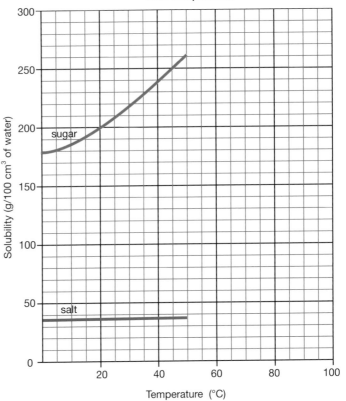

Graph to show how the solubility of sugar increases with temperature

7 Why does sugar dissolve better in hot tea than in cold water?

8 A saturated solution of benzoic acid has been made in hot water. As the water cools, crystals of benzoic acid are seen to form. Why is this?

FACT Gases also dissolve in liquids but they get less soluble as temperature increases. Fish in streams and ponds often die in very hot weather because there is too little oxygen in the water.

C9: Simple chemical reactions

In this unit you will learn to answer these questions:

▶ What is a chemical reaction?

▶ How do acids react with metals?

▶ How do acids react with carbonates?

Get started

What's the difference between what happens in these two diagrams?

When ice melts it doesn't change substance – it's still water and you can turn it back into ice. This is a **physical change** since no new substances are formed. It is also a **reversible change** because you can reverse it!

When an egg is fried, the yolk and the white change colour. New substances form and so this is a **chemical reaction**. It is also an **irreversible change** because you can't change the cooked egg back into raw egg.

In a chemical reaction new substances are formed. Things that tell you a chemical reaction is happening include: changes of colour, bubbles of gas, the substances getting hot or a flame appearing.

In a chemical reaction, you start with **reactants** and you end with **products**.

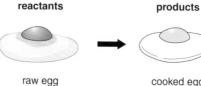

reactants   products

raw egg   cooked egg

FACT The reaction between hydrogen and oxygen is used in rockets.

Some reactions need help to get started. If you mix hydrogen gas with oxygen nothing happens. If you put a flame to them, they explode with a squeak.

Some reactions don't need help to get started. If you mix carbon dioxide gas with **limewater**, the limewater goes milky.

Practice

1 What is the difference between a chemical reaction and a physical change?

2 When you add hydrochloric acid to calcium metal, the metal bubbles. Why?

3 Which of these is the odd one out and why?

water → steam   potato → crisp   wood → ash   bread → toast

When a strip of magnesium metal is dropped into an acid, bubbles appear. Eventually the metal disappears. A chemical reaction has occurred in which the acid has **corroded** the metal. Many metals react with acids in this way.

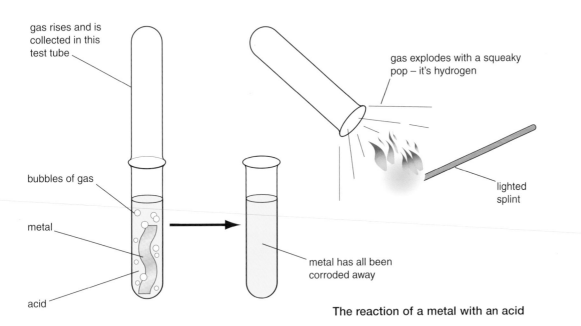

gas rises and is collected in this test tube

gas explodes with a squeaky pop – it's hydrogen

bubbles of gas

lighted splint

metal

metal has all been corroded away

acid

The reaction of a metal with an acid

The bubbles are caused by a gas being produced. If we collect this gas and put a lighted splint to it, the gas explodes with a squeak. This tells us that the gas is hydrogen. Putting a lighted splint to a gas is the test for hydrogen.

Acids also corrode substances called **carbonates**. Limestone is a carbonate. When an acid is added to limestone it fizzes. If we collect the gas and then mix the gas with limewater, the limewater goes milky. This tells us that the gas is carbon dioxide. Mixing a gas with limewater is the test for carbon dioxide. Carbon dioxide, like some other gases, will also put out a lighted splint.

Saying things out loud can help things stick in your brain. Try repeating: 'Acid plus metal produces hydrogen' and 'Acid plus carbonate produces carbon dioxide'.

FACT Fossil hunters get fossils out of limestone by corroding the limestone away with acid.

Practice

4 Name one product when hydrochloric acid reacts with magnesium metal.

5 Name one product when sulfuric acid reacts with limestone.

6 a What is the test for hydrogen?

   b What is the test for carbon dioxide?

7 An acid is added to limestone and bubbles of gas are collected. A lighted splint is put to the gas. What do you think happens?

C10: Burning

In this unit you will learn to answer these questions:

▸ What new substances are made when materials burn in air or oxygen?

▸ What is produced when fuels burn?

▸ What is needed for things to burn?

Get started

Burning wood is a chemical reaction. Draw a diagram of this chemical reaction. Label your diagram to show how you know it's a chemical reaction.

Some metals burn when they are heated in air. For example magnesium burns with a bright white flame.

Burning (properly called **combustion**) is a chemical reaction. In the case of magnesium one of the reactants is magnesium and the other is oxygen from the air. The product is an oxide called magnesium oxide.

We can show this as a **word equation**:

$$\text{magnesium} + \text{oxygen} \longrightarrow \text{magnesium oxide}$$

For combustion to occur you need heat, a **fuel** and oxygen. The air contains 20% oxygen. Things burn much better in 100% oxygen.

Remember the three things needed for combustion using the 'fire triangle' shown here.

Practice

1 How can you tell that burning magnesium is a chemical reaction?

2 The flame from burning magnesium is brighter in pure oxygen. Why?

3 Calcium will also burn in air. Write a word equation for this reaction.

A fuel is something that contains a store of energy that can be turned into heat energy, usually by burning.

Wood, candle wax, natural gas, coal, petrol and oil are all fuels. These fuels all contain carbon, so when they combust carbon dioxide is produced.

They also all contain hydrogen, so when they combust hydrogen oxide (more commonly called water!) is produced.

The general word equation looks like this:

fuel + oxygen ⟶ carbon dioxide + water

Natural gas is mainly **methane**. The word equation for burning natural gas is:

methane + oxygen ⟶ carbon dioxide + water

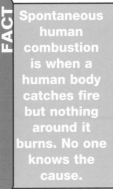
In an experiment, a candle was placed in a trough of water and lit. Then a jar was placed over it. The water rose inside the jar and the candle went out.

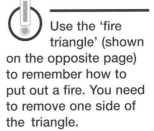

10 cm

6 seconds

2 cm

The candle went out because it had run out of oxygen. To put out a fire you need to take away the oxygen (air) or the fuel or the heat.

Use the 'fire triangle' (shown on the opposite page) to remember how to put out a fire. You need to remove one side of the triangle.

Practice

4 What is a fuel?

5 Candle wax is made of carbon and hydrogen. Write out a word equation for the combustion of candle wax.

6 a In the above experiment, why did the candle go out?

b Explain why the water rose 2 cm up the jar.

7 Why will water put out a bonfire?

8 Write a word equation for the combustion of hydrogen.

In this unit you will learn to answer these questions:

- How do we get other materials from elements?
- How can we represent the changes when new materials are made?

Get started

When there's a chemical reaction between magnesium (Mg) and sulfur (S) you end up with magnesium sulfide. How would you write magnesium sulfide in chemical symbols?

During a **chemical reaction** new substances are made. These new substances (the **products**) contain the same atoms as the materials you started with (the **reactants**) but joined together in different ways. Here's an example – the reaction between hydrogen gas and oxygen gas.

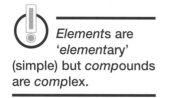

Elements are *'elementary'* (simple) but *comp*ounds are *complex*.

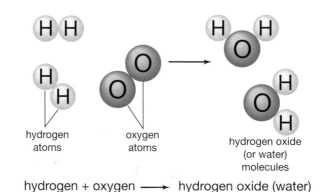

hydrogen atoms   oxygen atoms   hydrogen oxide (or water) molecules

hydrogen + oxygen ⟶ hydrogen oxide (water)

Oxygen is an element made of **molecules**. A molecule is a group of two or more atoms chemically joined together to form a bigger particle. Oxygen has two atoms of oxygen in its molecules. Water is a **compound** – it has more than one type of atom in its molecules. Each water molecule contains two hydrogen atoms joined to one oxygen atom.

Practice

1 You have been asked to write some definitions for a dictionary. Write down definitions for:

a a molecule

b an element

c a compound.

2 Oxygen exists as molecules. Name another element that exists as molecules.

3 Describe these molecules of different compounds:

a carbon dioxide   b hydrogen chloride

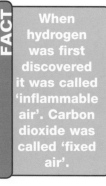

FACT

When hydrogen was first discovered it was called 'inflammable air'. Carbon dioxide was called 'fixed air'.

When materials react with oxygen they form **oxides**. Here's another example:

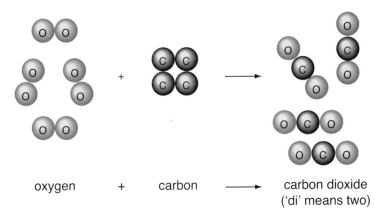

oxygen   +   carbon   ⟶   carbon dioxide
('di' means two)

Notice that there are the same number of atoms on each side of the arrow – in a chemical reaction you can't destroy the atoms, only rearrange them.

Rather than writing a **word equation**, we can write a **symbol equation**.

$$O_2 + C \longrightarrow CO_2$$

When a compound is written in symbols it's called a **chemical formula**. The little numbers after each symbol tell you how many of each sort of atom there are (if there are no numbers, there is only one atom). Some elements, like oxygen, always exist in molecules of two atoms and so they have the chemical formula O_2. Carbon can exist as single atoms.

Atoms aren't created or destroyed, they're merely redeployed.

Practice

4 What do you think will be formed when zinc reacts with oxygen?

5 Name two oxides.

6 Which of these are compounds?

O_2 $CaCl_2$ F_2 Fe   HCl   KF   Ne

7 Which elements are in the compound: $CaMg(CO_3)_2$?

8 Hydrogen reacts with chlorine.

  a Write out a word equation for this reaction.

  b Write out a symbol equation for this reaction. Chlorine gas exists in molecules of two chlorine atoms joined together. The product is HCl.

  c Draw a diagram to show how the atoms join.

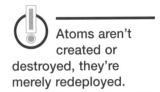

C12: Compounds

In this unit you will learn to answer these questions:

▶ How are elements and compounds different?

▶ How do compounds differ from the elements from which they are made?

▶ Do compounds react chemically?

Get started

Copy these molecules (there's no need to colour them in!). Write the correct chemical formula next to each drawing. Then circle the ones that are compounds.

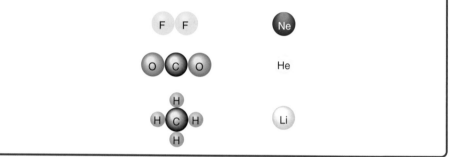

Iron and sulfur are **elements**. Grey iron powder is attracted to a magnet. Yellow sulfur powder is not. If you put iron powder in water it sinks. If you put sulfur powder in water it floats.

Some grey iron powder is mixed with some yellow sulfur powder and heated. A red glow spreads through the mixed powders. After it cools, a black solid is left which sinks in water and is not attracted to a magnet.

There has been a chemical reaction. We know this because there was a red glow and the properties of the **products** are not the same as the **reactants**. A new **compound** has been formed. Here are the equations:

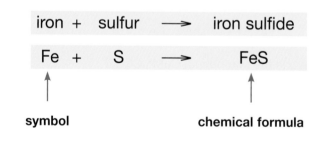

| iron | + | sulfur | ⟶ | iron sulfide |
| Fe | + | S | ⟶ | FeS |

symbol   chemical formula

Practice

1 Which properties of iron sulfide are different from the properties of sulfur?

2 What product is formed when iron reacts with sulfur?

The chemical formula FeS tells you that in iron sulfide there is always one iron atom for each sulfur atom. However, compounds that contain metals don't form molecules. Instead they form large blocks of atoms all joined together in a regular pattern.

The chemical formula of iron sulfide is always FeS. There is another compound of iron and sulfur, which has the formula FeS_2. This is iron disulfide and is a different compound with different properties.

It's not just elements that react. Compounds can react with elements (for example burning methane) and compounds can react with each other.

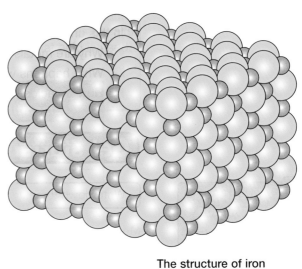

The structure of iron sulfide

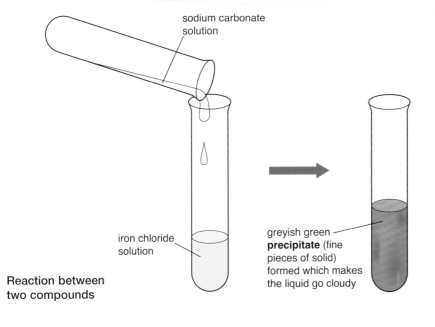

sodium carbonate solution

iron chloride solution

greyish green **precipitate** (fine pieces of solid) formed which makes the liquid go cloudy

Reaction between two compounds

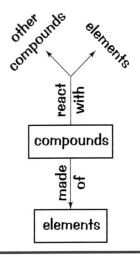

Draw a concept map for all the words in bold on these two pages. You could start like this:

Practice

3 Which of the following exist as molecules and which exist as blocks of atoms?

carbon dioxide   hydrogen chloride   sodium chloride

iron sulfide   silver oxide   hydrogen oxide

4 a When you mix sodium carbonate solution and iron chloride solution, how can you tell that there is a chemical reaction?

b Name one other way of telling that a chemical reaction is occurring.

5 What is a precipitate?

6 The chemical formula for iron chloride is $FeCl_2$. How many chlorine atoms are there for every iron atom in this compound?

C14: More salts

In this unit you will learn to answer these questions:

- What evidence is there of a chemical reaction between acids and metal oxides?
- What is a salt?

Get started

Why is 'common salt' a better name for the stuff that you put on your chips, rather than just 'salt'?

Another group of metal compounds are **metal oxides**. These all react with acids in similar ways too. The general reaction is:

metal oxide + acid ⟶ salt + water

Examples:

copper oxide	+	sulfuric acid	⟶	copper sulfate	+	water
CuO	+	H_2SO_4	⟶	$CuSO_4$	+	H_2O

magnesium oxide	+	hydrochloric acid	⟶	magnesium chloride	+	water
MgO	+	$2HCl$	⟶	$MgCl_2$	+	H_2O

Metal compounds that react with acids are called **bases**. Metal carbonates and metal oxides are both bases. The **solutions** that they produce when they react with acids (e.g. copper sulfate dissolved in water) are pH 7 (**neutral**) and these reactions are examples of **neutralisation**.

FACT

Most powdered metal oxides look dull but some can form crystals. Rubies and sapphires are mainly aluminium oxide.

Practice

1. Complete these word equations:

   a zinc oxide + hydrochloric acid →

   b magnesium oxide + sulfuric acid →

2. What metal oxide and what acid would you need to make:

   a copper chloride

   b magnesium nitrate

   c zinc sulfate

   d calcium chloride?

A base that is **soluble** in water is called an **alkali**. Alkalis end in the word 'hydroxide'. The general reaction for alkalis and acids is:

$$\text{acid} + \text{alkali} \longrightarrow \text{salt} + \text{water}$$

Examples:

potassium hydroxide + hydrochloric acid $\longrightarrow$ potassium chloride + water

$\quad$ KOH $\quad$ + $\quad$ HCl $\quad \longrightarrow \quad$ KCl $\quad$ + $\quad$ H_2O

sodium hydroxide + sulfuric acid $\longrightarrow$ sodium sulfate + water

$\quad$ 2NaOH $\quad$ + $\quad$ H_2SO_4 $\quad \longrightarrow \quad$ Na_2SO_4 $\quad$ + $\quad$ $2H_2O$

Notice that the name of a salt always has two parts. The first is the name of the metal in the base and the second is from the acid.

Salts have many uses. For example, copper sulfate is used to kill fungi, potassium nitrate is used in fireworks and sodium chloride is used to improve the taste of food.

You must be careful when making and handling salts. Some salts are poisonous (toxic) and the acids and bases used to make them can be harmful or corrosive. Wash off any chemicals that you get on your skin with plenty of water and always wear eye protection.

Construct a concept map to show the reactions of metals and bases with acids.

FACT There are other salts too, formed from different acids. Sodium stearate is used in soap and calcium phosphate is the main substance in our bones and teeth.

Practice

3. What is neutralisation?

4. What pH does a neutral solution have?

5. a What pH does a solution of sodium chloride in water have?

   b What acid and what alkali would you use to make this solution?

   c How would you stay safe when you add these two liquids together?

6. Copy and complete these word equations:

   a sodium + nitric acid $\longrightarrow$? + ?

   b potassium hydroxide + ? $\longrightarrow$ potassium chloride + water

   c ? + sulfuric acid $\longrightarrow$ calcium sulfate + carbon dioxide + ?

   d copper oxide + ? $\longrightarrow$ copper chloride + ?

   e ? + ? $\longrightarrow$ potassium chloride + hydrogen

   f ? + nitric acid $\longrightarrow$ zinc nitrate + ? + water

   g magnesium + hydrochloric acid $\longrightarrow$? + ?

C15: Reactivity

In this unit you will learn to answer these questions:
- Why do metals tarnish?
- How do metals react with water?
- Is the order of reactivity of metals with water the same as that with acids?

Get started

Write a list of things that go rusty. What are they all made of?

Many metals lose their shine – they **tarnish**. Over time iron rusts, copper turns black or green and silver becomes dirty looking. Some metals only take a few minutes to tarnish (e.g. sodium). Other metals don't tarnish (e.g. gold). Tarnishing is caused by the metal reacting with gases in the air or with water.

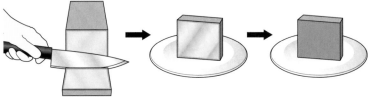

Sodium is a very soft metal that can be cut with a knife.

The freshly cut surface is shiny.

After a couple of minutes the cut surface is dull grey.

Write down all the general reactions on pages 81–84. Learn them until you can write them all out from memory without any mistakes.

Some metals react quickly with water. Calcium fizzes in water and gives off hydrogen gas. If you test the solution left behind with **universal indicator**, it turns blue, showing that an alkali has been formed. The alkali formed when calcium reacts with water is calcium hydroxide. The general reaction is:

$$\text{metal + water} \longrightarrow \text{metal hydroxide + hydrogen}$$

FACT Copper roofs go green naturally over a period of about 10 years but today they are often treated to make them go green faster.

Practice

1. Why do metals tarnish?

2. Name a metal that tarnishes quickly.

3. Write out the word equation for the reaction between calcium and water.

Some metals react with water faster than others.

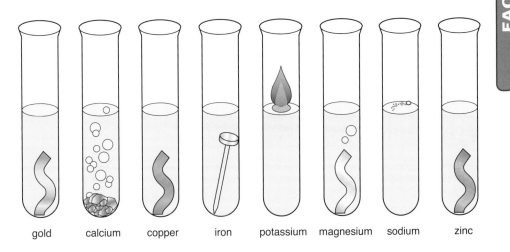

gold   calcium   copper   iron   potassium   magnesium   sodium   zinc

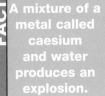
Potassium is the most **reactive** – the reaction causes the metal to catch fire. Next is sodium (the hydrogen gas is released so quickly that the metal can't sink), then calcium and then magnesium.

If the metals are reacted with acid, the order of reactivity is the same. However, zinc and iron react with acids although they don't react very quickly with water. Zinc reacts faster than iron.

The general reaction is:

$$\text{metal + acid} \longrightarrow \text{salt + hydrogen}$$

A list of the metals in order of reactivity is called the **reactivity series**. You don't need to remember it!

potassium

sodium

calcium

magnesium

zinc

iron

copper

gold

increasing reactivity

The reactivity series

Practice

4 Look at the diagrams at the top of the page.

a Which metal is the most reactive?

b How can you tell?

c Which metals are not reacting (or reacting so slowly that you can't see)?

d How can you tell?

e What are the bubbles made out of?

f What is the solution left behind after potassium has finished reacting?

5 What is the reactivity series?

C16: Using the reactivity series

In this unit you will learn to answer these questions:

▶ Can metals displace each other?

▶ How does the reactivity series relate to the uses and sources of metals?

Get started

Metals are added to acid: metal X produces lots of bubbles, metal Y catches fire, metal Z does nothing. Write an order of reactivity for the metals with the most reactive first.

Metals react with oxygen in the air to form metal **oxides**:

$$\text{metal} + \text{oxygen} \longrightarrow \text{metal oxide}$$

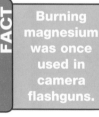

FACT Burning magnesium was once used in camera flashguns.

Magnesium burns in air with a bright white flame. If copper is heated it turns black. The flame shows that magnesium is more reactive than copper. The order of reactivity for heating metals in air is the same as in the reactivity series.

If magnesium and copper oxide are heated together, the magnesium pulls the oxygen away from the copper, forming magnesium oxide and copper metal. This is a **displacement reaction**. A metal that is higher than another in the reactivity series will displace ('kick out') a lower metal from its compounds. This is most often seen when metals are added to solutions of metal salts.

Magnesium burning in air

Examples:

$$\text{iron} + \text{copper sulfate} \longrightarrow \text{iron sulfate} + \text{copper}$$

$$\text{magnesium} + \text{zinc chloride} \longrightarrow \text{magnesium chloride} + \text{zinc}$$

But:

$$\text{copper} + \text{iron nitrate} \longrightarrow \text{NO REACTION}$$

Practice

① What is formed when magnesium burns in air?

② What is a displacement reaction?

③ Why is there no reaction when copper is added to iron nitrate solution?

The reactivity of metals affects their uses. Calcium isn't used for knives and forks because it would react with the water in food. Magnesium is light but isn't used for aircraft since it reacts with rainwater. Gold isn't used in fireworks because it doesn't react with the air when heated.

Unreactive metals were the first to be discovered. Ancient peoples knew about gold and silver because these metals were found in their natural states. Copper and iron, which are easy to extract from their natural compounds by heating with charcoal, were discovered about 3000–5000 years ago.

Reactive metals are very difficult to separate from their natural compounds and it often takes a lot of electricity to extract them. These metals have therefore been discovered more recently. Pure potassium was first obtained in 1807 and aluminium in 1825.

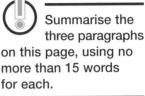
Summarise the three paragraphs on this page, using no more than 15 words for each.

Practice

4 Copy and complete these equations. Some may *not* react, in which case write 'no reaction'.

a zinc + iron sulfate $\longrightarrow$

b magnesium + sodium chloride $\longrightarrow$

c potassium + copper nitrate $\longrightarrow$

d calcium + copper sulfate $\longrightarrow$

5 Why is magnesium not found in its natural state?

6 Why is sodium not used to make car bodies?

7 Look at the reactivity series on page 85. Which metals do you think were discovered in the nineteenth century? Why do you think this?

8 Some magnesium was added to hydrochloric acid. The temperature was measured. The graph on the right shows the results.

a Write out a word equation for the reaction.

b How does the graph tell you that a reaction is happening?

c Why does the graph level off after about a minute?

d Why does the temperature fall after about 2 minutes?

e What do you think the temperature will be after 30 minutes?

f If calcium was used instead of magnesium what difference would there be in the experiment? Explain your answer.

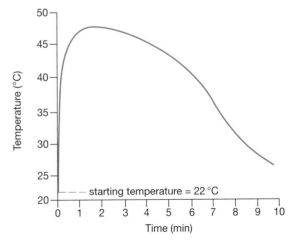

The change in temperature as magnesium is added to hydrochloric acid

starting temperature = 22 °C

9 Metal X reacts with copper sulfate solution but not with zinc chloride solution. Metal Y reacts with both solutions. Write out a reactivity series for Metals X, Y, zinc and copper with the most reactive first.

C17: Chemical reactions for energy

In this unit you will learn to answer these questions:
▶ What chemical reactions take place when fuels burn?
▶ How else are chemical reactions used as energy resources?

Get started

Which of these are fuels?

coal   hydrogen   natural gas   oil   petrol   wood

A **fuel** contains stored energy that can be turned into heat energy, usually by burning. Most fuels are **hydrocarbons** (made of carbon and hydrogen) and **combust** to form carbon dioxide and water.

$$\text{methane} + \text{oxygen} \longrightarrow \text{carbon dioxide} + \text{water}$$

If there's not enough oxygen, soot (carbon) and carbon monoxide are formed.

$$\text{methane} + \text{oxygen} \longrightarrow \text{carbon monoxide} + \text{carbon} + \text{water}$$

Methane burning in a lack of oxygen

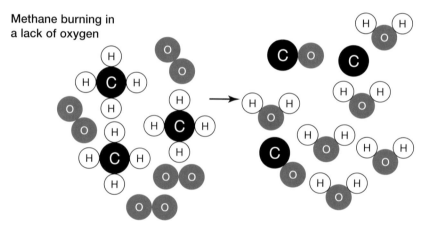

Hydrogen can be used as a fuel. It's light and doesn't form carbon dioxide when burnt. It is used to power some rockets. However, it needs to be compressed in tanks to store it and is highly explosive when mixed with air.

$$\text{hydrogen} + \text{oxygen} \longrightarrow \text{water}$$

Practice

1 How would you find out if burning methane produced carbon dioxide?

2 'All cars should run on hydrogen.' Give one reason why this would be good, one reason why it would be bad, and find out an interesting fact about hydrogen.

3 Write down the chemical formulae for:

a carbon monoxide

b soot.

Apart from combustion, other chemical reactions can be used as energy resources.

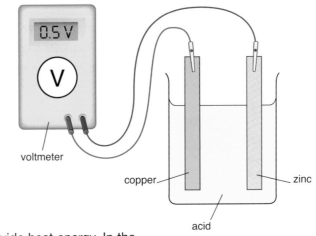

voltmeter

copper   zinc

acid

If two different metals are dipped into an acid and connected with a wire, a voltage will be produced. The greater the difference in reactivity between the two metals, the greater the voltage.

Displacement reactions can also provide heat energy. In the **thermit reaction** powdered aluminium and iron oxide are mixed and lit. The reaction produces so much heat that molten iron is formed. This reaction is used to join railway tracks together.

Other displacement reactions using a metal and a solution of a metal salt also produce heat energy. For example:

zinc + copper sulfate ⟶ zinc sulfate + copper

(solution)   (solution)

The greater the difference between the reactivity of the metal and the metal in the salt, the more heat produced.

Practice

4 Carbon monoxide is a poisonous gas. Why do you think that gas fires need to be checked each year to make sure that enough air is getting into them?

5 a Which of these pairs of metals will produce the greatest voltage when connected up as shown in the diagram at the top of the page?

    A iron and copper

    B iron and gold

    C zinc and gold

    D zinc and copper

    E zinc and iron

  b What sort of energy is being produced in this experiment?

6 Write out the word equation for the thermit reaction.

7 a Copy and complete these equations. (*Hint:* Look back at page 86 for help.)

    i zinc + iron chloride ⟶

    ii gold + zinc sulfate ⟶

    iii zinc + copper nitrate ⟶

  b What sort of reactions are these?

  c Which reaction would produce the most heat energy?

FACT

In the UK, about 50 people are killed each year by carbon monoxide produced by faulty gas fires and boilers.

In this unit you will learn to answer these questions:

▶ What types of new material are made through chemical reactions?

▶ What happens to atoms and molecules when new materials are made?

Get started

Which of these materials have been made by chemical reactions?

cellulose (found in plant cell walls)   glass   hair   paint   plastic

All the compounds around us have been made by chemical reactions. Some are made by chemical reactions in living things and others by chemical reactions in laboratories and factories.

Scientists try to develop new materials (e.g. new medicines, new plastics). They find natural materials and work out how to make them in a lab or they react chemicals together to try to create new materials with certain properties.

All materials made in chemical reactions are formed by combining atoms from the reactants in different ways. Atoms aren't made or destroyed.

Atoms aren't made or destroyed during chemical reactions – they are rearranged

⚠ Learn the sentence 'mass is neither created nor destroyed' off by heart. It's called the **law of conservation of mass** and is very important.

Since the types of and the numbers of different atoms in a reaction do not change, the mass of the reactants is equal to the mass of the products. Mass is neither created nor destroyed.

Practice

❶ Why do scientists want to develop new materials? Give one example.

❷ What does the 'law of conservation of mass' say?

❸ Write out word equations for the three reactions shown in the diagrams above.

In an investigation some students measured the masses of some pieces of magnesium and then burned them in air. The graph shows their results. You can see that magnesium oxide always has a greater mass than the magnesium at the start. This extra mass has come from the oxygen in the air.

When you burn a candle, mass appears to be lost since the candle gets smaller. In fact, the mass of the reactants and the mass of the products are the same, it's just that the products are gases that drift away from the candle.

Graph to show mass of magnesium oxide produced when magnesium is burned in air

The masses of the reactants and products when burning candle wax are the same

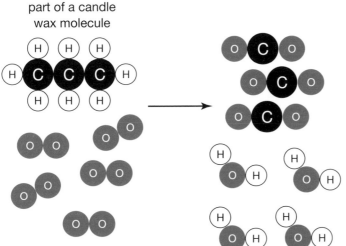

part of a candle
wax molecule

candle wax + oxygen ⟶ carbon dioxide + water
(a hydrocarbon)

It's sometimes difficult to think of gases having a mass, but they all do. Remember: 'A gas has mass'.

Until the eighteenth century, scientists could not understand why some materials seemed to lose mass when they burned. To explain it, they invented the **phlogiston theory** (pronounced '*flo-jiss-ton*'). This theory said that materials contain a substance called phlogiston and that they lose this substance when burned.

Practice

4 a Write out a word equation for the reaction shown in the *graph*.

   b Why does magnesium appear to get heavier when burned in air?

   c How much magnesium oxide is produced by 10 g of magnesium?

5 If you hold a cold tile above a candle flame, a liquid condenses on it. What is this liquid?

6 a What was the phlogiston theory?

   b How did this theory explain why wood loses mass when it burns?

   c Which of the reactions on this page can the phlogiston theory not explain?

C19: Rocks and weathering

In this unit you will learn to answer these questions:

▶ What are rocks made of?

▶ How does rain cause rocks to weather?

▶ How do changes in temperature cause rocks to weather?

Get started

Think of a rock that you've seen. Write down how you would describe it to someone who hadn't seen it.

 *Sandstone has Smooth grains, gran/te has /nterlocking cr/stals.*

Rocks are made of tiny **grains** of compounds called **minerals**. Different rocks are made of different minerals, giving each one its colour. You need a microscope to see a rock's **texture** – the shapes and sizes of its grains and how they fit together.

rounded mineral grains

gap

Sandstone seen through a microscope

Rocks like **sandstone** are made of rounded grains that do not fit together and have gaps between them. A rock like this is said to be **porous** because water can flow slowly through it, in the spaces between the grains.

Rocks like **granite** have an **interlocking texture**. They are made of grains with sharp edges (called **crystals**) that all fit together. Rocks like this are not porous.

three different minerals

interlocking crystals

Granite seen through a microscope

Practice

1 What are rocks made of?

2 Describe the texture of sandstone.

3 What is a crystal?

4 Two rocks are put into water. Bubbles come out of rock A but not rock B. Which rock is sandstone? Explain how you worked this out.

IN LOVING MEMORY OF DAVID PORTER

1932 - 2000

Which is the older of these two gravestones?

Rocks that are outside get worn away. This is called **weathering**.

Rain contains dissolved gases from the air, like carbon dioxide, which make it acidic (about pH 6). The acid reacts with minerals. The products dissolve in the rain water and are washed away. This is called **chemical weathering**.

Porous rocks, like limestone and sandstone, weather more quickly than non-porous rocks because the rain gets inside them.

Physical weathering is when rock is weathered by **physical changes**, like temperature changes. As a rock heats up, it **expands**. When it cools down again it **contracts**, causing forces inside the rock that crack it.

A mnemonic for the different types of weathering (biological, chemical, physical) is: 'Britain's Currency's Pounds'. You can probably think up a better one!

Changes in temperature often make rocks 'peel'

If water gets into cracks in rocks and freezes, it expands and cracks the rock further. When the ice melts, the water runs into the rest of the crack. If it freezes again it will make the crack even bigger. This is **freeze–thaw action**.

Plant roots can grow in the cracks in a rock and make the cracks bigger as they grow. Weathering caused by living things is **biological weathering**.

FACT Water expands by about 10% when it turns to ice.

Practice

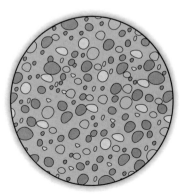

5 a What is weathering?

b What are the three main types of weathering?

6 Which rock will be chemically weathered more quickly – sandstone or granite? Explain your answer.

7 Describe the texture of the rock on the right.

8 Draw a set of diagrams to explain what happens in freeze–thaw action.

C20: Erosion and deposition

In this unit you will learn to answer these questions:

▶ What happens to weathered pieces of rock?

▶ Why do sediments form layers?

Get started

Scientists measured the speed of water in various rivers and the diameters of rocks carried by the water. The graph shows some of their results.

Complete this sentence to say what the graph shows: 'The faster the water, the bigger...'

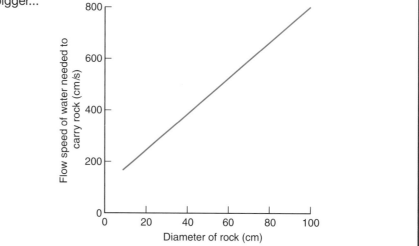

Rocks are broken apart by **weathering** into rock fragments. When these fragments are carried away by water, air or ice it is called **erosion**.

Flowing water carries rock fragments. The faster the water flows, the heavier the fragments it can carry. As the fragments travel they bump into one another and wear away. This is called **abrasion**. The longer the fragments are carried, the more they are abraded.

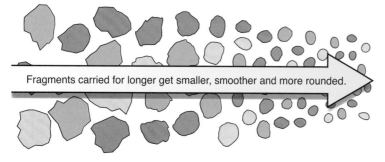

Fragments carried for longer get smaller, smoother and more rounded.

Abrasion of rock fragments in flowing water

The bits of rock carried by a river or stream are called **sediment**. When a river slows down, the sediment falls to the bottom – it is **deposited**.

Practice

1 What is erosion?

2 Here's a diagram looking down at a river. The water flows more slowly near the banks of the river.

Suggest why there are large stones at the edges of the river but not in the middle.

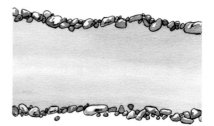

When a river flows out to sea or into a lake, the water slows down and the sediments are deposited. In time, layers of sediment build up. The river may have been flowing faster at some times than others and so some layers of sediment may contain larger rock fragments than other layers.

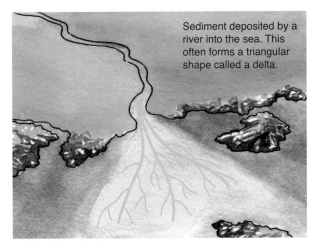

Sediment deposited by a river into the sea. This often forms a triangular shape called a delta.

A river delta

The upper layers of sediment push down on the lower layers, which eventually turn into rock, although this may take millions of years. Rocks formed from sediment are **sedimentary rocks** and examples include **sandstone** (made from sand), **mudstone** (made from fine grains) and **conglomerate** (made from pebbles).

Layers can also be formed in other ways:

- when seawater evaporates leaving dissolved solids behind (salt)

- when the shells of sea creatures collect on the sea floor (**limestone**)

- when dead plants are squashed under other layers (coal)

- when dead sea organisms are squashed under other layers (oil and natural gas).

FACT Limestone has many uses – including in cement, in glass and in toothpaste!

Practice

3 The layers of rock shown here were originally formed when sediment flowed into the sea from a river.

a Which layer was deposited when the river was flowing fastest?

b Which is the oldest layer?

c What type of rock could layer B be?

4 Salt is mined underground in Cheshire. Suggest how it came to be there.

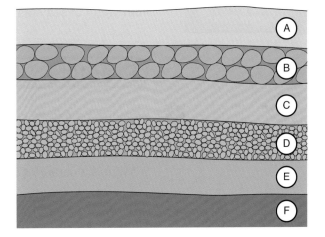

C21: Sedimentary and metamorphic rocks

In this unit you will learn to answer these questions:
- How is sedimentary rock formed?
- Are all limestones the same?
- What is different about metamorphic rocks?

Get started

This page contains many words from the previous two units. Write a list of all the words in bold on this page and make sure you can say what each one means. If you don't know one, look up its meaning in the glossary.

Write down a list of the names of some rocks you have heard of. Keep your list.

Sedimentary rocks are formed from **sediments** (**weathered** rock fragments carried by rivers) that are **deposited** in layers. As new layers are deposited on top of old layers, the old layers are put under pressure and squashed. Water is squeezed out from between the grains (**compaction**).

As the water is squeezed out, minerals dissolved in the water are left behind and form a 'glue' that sticks the grains together. This is called **cementation**.

FACT

The biggest fish ever found is a fossil unearthed in a layer of clay near Peterborough. It is over 22 metres long – twice as long as today's biggest fish.

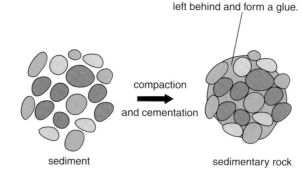

Mineral salts from water get left behind and form a glue.

compaction and cementation

sediment

sedimentary rock

How sedimentary rocks are formed

Most sedimentary rocks are **porous** and some contain **fossils**. **Limestones** can contain fossils, depending on how they were formed. Some limestones were formed from prehistoric coral reefs, some were formed from calcium carbonate being left behind by water as it evaporated and some were formed from layers of sea creature shells. The last type often contains fossils.

Practice

1 What two processes turn layers of sediment into rock?

2 a Name three ways in which limestone can be formed.

b What is a coral reef? If you don't know, find out.

All limestones are **carbonate-rich** because they are made mainly of compounds called carbonates (mostly calcium carbonate). Calcium carbonate is white but limestones can be different colours due to impurities, like mud, getting into the sediment layers before they turn to rock.

Type of limestone	Percentage carbonate	How it formed
chalk	99	from tiny shells and skeletons of dead sea animals (e.g. those in a coral reef)
coquina	95	from larger shells
oolite	85	from calcium carbonate left behind by evaporating water

All carbonates react with acids (see pages 72–73). The more carbonates in limestone, the more it will react with an acid.

If sedimentary rocks get buried deep in the Earth they can be changed by the very high temperatures and/or pressures found there. The rocks turn into **metamorphic rocks**.

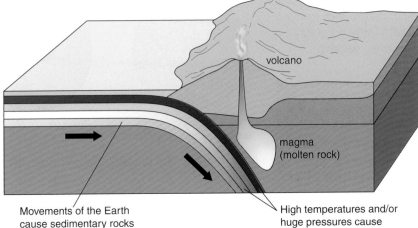

volcano

magma (molten rock)

Movements of the Earth cause sedimentary rocks to become buried.

High temperatures and/or huge pressures cause metamorphic rocks to form.

How metamorphic rocks are formed

When metamorphic rocks form, the sedimentary grains can turn into **interlocking crystals,** which often form bands or stripes in the rock. If fossils were in the original sedimentary rock these become strange, distorted shapes. Examples of metamorphic rocks include **marble** (formed from limestone) and **quartzite** (from sandstone).

FACT Rubies can be formed when limestone is changed into marble.

Practice

3 Look at the table above showing the limestones.

a They all fizz when acid is added to them. Why?

b If the same amount of acid is added to equal masses of each rock, which will fizz the longest?

c Which of these limestones is least likely to contain fossils?

4 What sedimentary rock is marble formed from?

5 a Are metamorphic rocks more or less porous than sedimentary rocks?

b Why is this?

C22: Igneous rocks

In this unit you will learn to answer these questions:
- ▶ Where do igneous rocks come from?
- ▶ What is the rock cycle?

Get started

Magma is molten rock. What do you think will happen when it cools?

Most of the Earth is made of molten rock called **magma** and this sometimes comes to the surface in volcanoes. When it cools, it forms **igneous rocks**.

Magma comes out of volcanoes as liquid **lava** or ash (when lava droplets have turned to solid). Ash sets hard to form rocks like **tuff**. Lava cools quickly. If it cools very quickly it forms rocks without **crystals** (**obsidian**). Otherwise the minerals solidify, forming rock with small crystals (e.g. **basalt**).

Sometimes magma cools more slowly underground, forming rocks with large crystals (e.g. **granite**, **gabbro**).

When cooling of magma is slow, large crystals form.

When cooling of magma is rapid, small crystals form.

The **density** of something is the mass that 1 cm³ of it has. Some igneous rocks contain lots of iron and are very dense (e.g. gabbro). Others contain a less dense mineral called silica (e.g. granite). The diagram below shows how to work out the density of a rock.

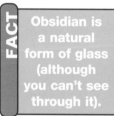

Remember how to calculate density using this triangle – cover up the D and it shows that you need to divide mass by volume. Think up a mnemonic to remember the order of letters (for example 'My Dented Van').

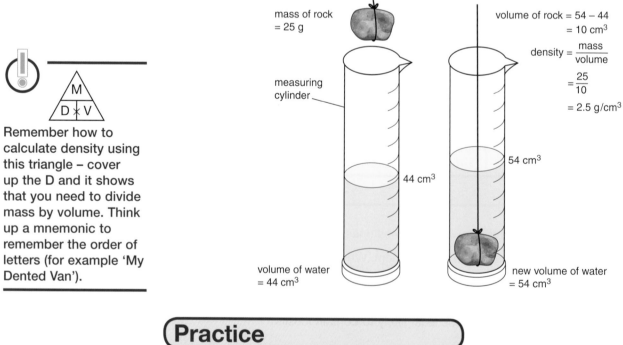

mass of rock = 25 g

measuring cylinder

volume of water = 44 cm³

44 cm³

54 cm³

new volume of water = 54 cm³

volume of rock = 54 − 44
= 10 cm³

$$\text{density} = \frac{\text{mass}}{\text{volume}}$$

$$= \frac{25}{10}$$

$$= 2.5 \text{ g/cm}^3$$

Practice

1 A rock has a volume of 40 cm³ and a mass of 120 g. What is its density?

2 What is the difference between lava and magma?

Igneous rocks can also be changed into metamorphic rocks. For example, granite can be turned into **gneiss** (pronounced 'nice').

All the different processes that make and change rocks can be shown in the **rock cycle**.

The rock cycle

Practice

3 Find the list of rocks that you made in the 'Get started' question on page 96.

a Add all the other names of rocks that you have met to your list.

b Write down whether each rock is sedimentary, metamorphic or igneous.

4 Write three sentences to summarise how each of the three main types of rocks are formed.

5 You examine some rocks using a hand lens. They look like this.

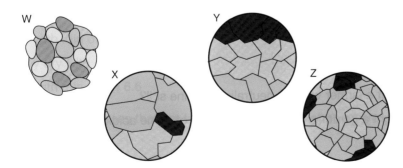

Say what you can about each rock.

C24: Pollution and global warming

In this unit you will learn to answer these questions:

▶ What are the effects of acid rain and how can they be reduced?

▶ Is pollution getting worse?

▶ Is global warming happening?

Get started

The writing on gravestones from the 1800s is much more readable in country churchyards than in city ones. Why do you think this is?

Acid rain **corrodes** metals and quickly weathers **sedimentary rocks** because they are **porous** and the acid rain gets inside them. **Limestone** rocks weather very quickly because the acid reacts with the carbonate that they contain. Acid rain weathers **igneous rocks** more slowly.

Acid rain kills plants by making the soil too acidic, and by reacting with and destroying the **mineral salts**. When acid rainwater gets into ponds and lakes it can make the water too acidic so that the animals and plants in it die. The bars on the chart below show the range of pHs that some water creatures can survive in.

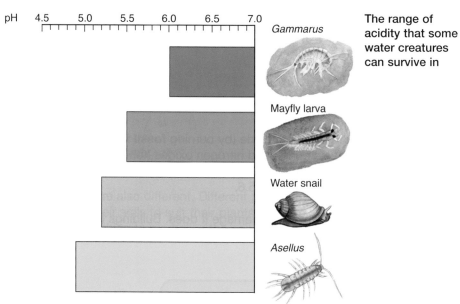

The range of acidity that some water creatures can survive in

Today, **sulfur precipitators** are fitted to power station and factory chimneys to take the sulfur dioxide out of their smoke. New cars are all fitted with **catalytic converters** that change nitrogen oxides into harmless nitrogen.

Practice

1 Why does limestone weather more quickly than sandstone?

2 A lake is affected by acid rain and its pH drops to pH 5.3. Which organisms in the chart above are likely to be able to survive in the lake?

3 What is the point of using sulfur precipitators and catalytic converters?

Pollution is when substances in an environment cause problems. Monitoring stations detect the levels of different gases in the air. Data from these stations can be found on the internet and show that in the last 40 years air pollution in towns and cities has been reduced.

Other evidence about how pollution is changing can be obtained from written reports about the weather going back hundreds of years, old photographs, paintings and records of diseases.

Although air pollution in cities seems to be getting less, scientists think that the atmosphere is heating up (**global warming**) due to increasing levels of gases like carbon dioxide and methane. These are **greenhouse gases**, which trap some of the Earth's heat that would otherwise escape into space.

Make a list of all the bold words on the last four pages and their meanings. You can use the glossary at the back of the book to help you with the meanings. Cover up the words and say what word each meaning is referring to.

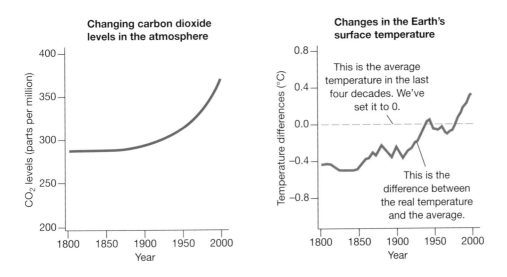

You can see from the graph on the right that the temperatures in the last few decades have been above average and are steadily rising.

Practice

4 What is air pollution?

5 a What does a greenhouse gas do?

b Name two examples of greenhouse gases.

6 a What is global warming?

b How do the two graphs provide evidence that carbon dioxide levels cause global warming?

7 How might an old photograph provide evidence for how air pollution levels have changed compared with today?

8 What could *you* do to help reduce pollution?

FACT

Sea levels have risen by about 10 cm in 100 years. Scientists think this is due to global warming and that, if nothing is done about it, London will be flooded by 2100.

In this unit you will learn to answer these questions:

▶ What are renewable energy resources?

▶ How do living things use energy?

Get started

Sort these energy resources into two groups. Give each group a title.

coal   geothermal   oil   Sun   water   wind   wood

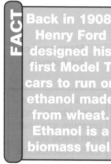

FACT Back in 1908, Henry Ford designed his first Model T cars to run on ethanol made from wheat. Ethanol is a biomass fuel.

Some of the things we use to provide us with energy (**energy resources**) are **renewable**, which means that they will not run out.

Wind turbines are driven by the wind and produce electricity. They turn movement energy of the wind into electrical energy. Wind doesn't run out!

Wood is used as fuel in many parts of the world. It can be re-grown so it is a renewable resource. Energy resources from living things are **biomass fuels**.

Solar panels use energy from the Sun to heat up water. **Solar cells** turn light energy from the Sun into electrical energy.

solar cells

Solar cells in a calculator

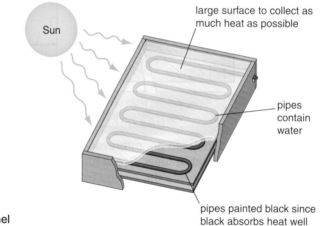

Sun

large surface to collect as much heat as possible

pipes contain water

pipes painted black since black absorbs heat well

Solar panel

Think up a mnemonic for the different renewable energy resources.

Heat from rocks deep underground can be used to heat water and make electricity. This is **geothermal power**.

The power of water held back by a dam can be used to turn **turbines**, which produce electricity. This is **hydroelectric power**.

Practice

1 What is a biomass fuel?

2 Why won't solar cells make electricity 24 hours a day?

3 Design a way to provide electricity for a town in the year 2050.

All living things need energy. Plants get their energy from the Sun. Animals get their energy from food.

Foods have **nutrition information** labels on them that tell us what is in them. These labels show how much 'energy' is in the food.

Energy is measured in **joules (J)**. One joule is about the amount of energy needed to raise a medium-sized apple by 1 metre. One **kilojoule** is 1000 joules. Calories are the old-fashioned units for energy.

The energy stored in food is called **chemical energy**. Your body turns this into other sorts of energy (e.g. **heat energy**, **movement energy**). You use more chemical energy when you exercise. The apparatus shown on page 104 is used to find out how much energy is in dry food.

Nutrition Information		
	Per 40 g serving	Per 100 g
Energy	506 kJ (121 kcal)	1265 kJ (302 kcal)
Protein	4.7 g	11.8 g
Carbohydrate	20.9 g	52.3 g
Fat	1.9 g	4.7 g
Fibre	9.9 g	24.8 g
Sodium	0.2 g	0.5 g

Plants make their own food. They turn **light energy** from the Sun into chemical energy, which is stored in substances like starch. We get this chemical energy when we eat the plants!

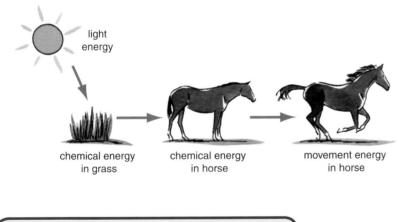

light energy

chemical energy in grass   chemical energy in horse   movement energy in horse

Practice

4 Where do you get your energy from?

5 Look at the nutrition label above.

  a How much energy is in 100 g of this food?

  b How many apples could you raise by 1 m if you ate 40 g of the food?

6 Draw a flow diagram, like the one above, to show how you get energy to ride a bike from eating potatoes.

7 How could you find out which of two breakfast cereals contained more energy, without looking at the boxes?

FACT Fireflies produce light energy using the chemical energy in their food.

P4: Heating and cooling

In this unit you will learn to answer these questions:

▶ How do materials change when they are heated and cooled?
▶ How can we reduce energy waste?
▶ How can we explain changes of state?

Get started

A metal ball can just fit through a hoop. When the metal ball is heated it will no longer fit through the hoop. Why?

When a substance is heated, its particles vibrate more. As they vibrate more, they need more space to move around and so the substance gets bigger (it **expands**). Note that the particles themselves *do not* get bigger.

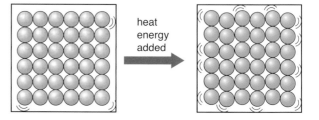

heat energy added

Expansion in a solid

When the substance cools, it gets smaller again – it **contracts**.

When a substance expands it takes up more room but has the same mass and so its density is less (see page 98). Things with lower densities float in liquids with higher densities.

The flow of a liquid or a gas due to part of it being heated is called a **convection current**. The heat is travelling from place to place by **convection**.

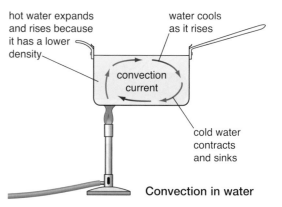

hot water expands and rises because it has a lower density

water cools as it rises

convection current

cold water contracts and sinks

Convection in water

FACT
There is often a breeze at the beach on a sunny day. This is a convection current caused by the ground being hotter than the sea and heating the air above it.

Heat travels through space from the Sun by **radiation**. It also travels through **transparent** things by radiation. Unlike convection and conduction, radiation does not need particles to carry the energy.

Practice

1 Why do things contract when they cool? Explain your answer in terms of particles.

2 List three ways in which heat energy can travel.

3 When small pasta pieces are being boiled, they seem to move up and down in the pan in circles. Why?

We use energy to heat our homes but heat can be lost again by conduction, convection and radiation. Houses with better insulation have lower energy bills because they lose less heat. Examples include double glazing, loft insulation and wall insulation. Most insulation relies on trapped air.

We also use energy in our homes to change things between different **states of matter**. These changes of state all rely on adding or removing heat energy. The graph shows what happens when ice is heated.

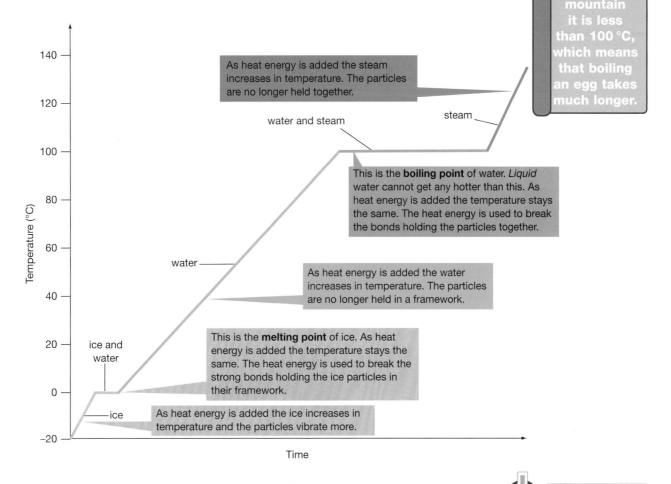

As heat energy is added the steam increases in temperature. The particles are no longer held together.

This is the **boiling point** of water. *Liquid water cannot get any hotter than this.* As heat energy is added the temperature stays the same. The heat energy is used to break the bonds holding the particles together.

As heat energy is added the water increases in temperature. The particles are no longer held in a framework.

This is the **melting point** of ice. As heat energy is added the temperature stays the same. The heat energy is used to break the strong bonds holding the ice particles in their framework.

As heat energy is added the ice increases in temperature and the particles vibrate more.

Practice

4 a Give an example of house insulation.

   b Explain how it works.

5 If you drop hot, melted wax on you it changes back into a solid … and hurts! Where does the heat energy go when the wax changes into a solid?

6 What are the three states of matter?

7 When ice is being heated, why does the temperature not rise until it has all become liquid?

Without looking back at the graph, shut the book and sketch the line of the graph and the axes. If you get it wrong take a closer look at it and then try again. This is a good way of quickly checking that you've taken something in.

P5: Light

In this unit you will learn to answer these questions:
- ▶ How does light travel?
- ▶ What happens when light meets an object?
- ▶ How do we see things?
- ▶ How do mirrors reflect light?
- ▶ How are images formed?

Get started

Use your hand to create a shadow. What did you need to create your shadow? Why does your shadow have a certain shape?

Light is produced by **luminous sources** (e.g. a light bulb) and travels very, very fast (over 1 billion kilometres per hour!).

Light travels in straight lines and we show this by drawing **light rays** on diagrams.

shadow on screen

suspended ball

light on screen

small hole in card

Shadows form because light cannot go round corners!

When light hits an object one of three things happens to it. It can be:

- ● **absorbed** – taken into the object (black things do this)
- ● **transmitted** – allowed through (transparent things do this)
- ● **reflected** – bounced off the object (most things do this).

Practice

1 Maria is looking down a tube at some grass.

a Why can't she see the grass?

b What must she do to see it?

c Why must she do this?

2 What happens to light when it hits:

a a piece of glass

b a clean blackboard?

We see light when it enters our eyes. Most things don't give out their own light and are **non-luminous** but we can see them because they reflect light.

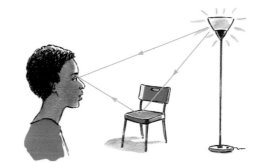

We can see non-luminous objects because they reflect light

Most things reflect light in all directions but very flat surfaces (e.g. mirrors) reflect light evenly, so we can see images in them. The angle at which a light ray hits a mirror is equal to the angle at which the light ray leaves the mirror (**angle of incidence = angle of reflection**).

When you look in a mirror you see an image in which left is right and right is left. Since light travels in straight lines, the image appears to come from behind the mirror.

Make a sketch of a light ray hitting an object. Then show the three different things that could happen to it. Label your diagram to make a complete summary of the information on these two pages.

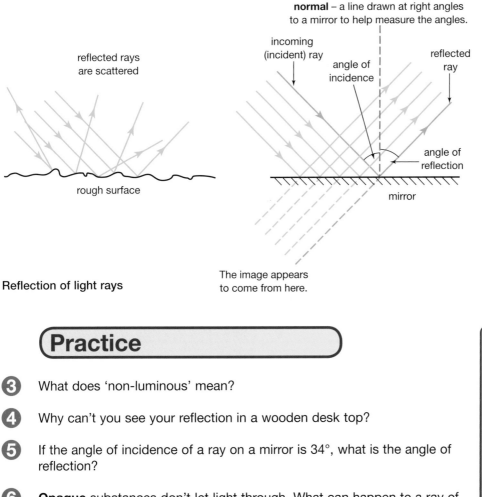

reflected rays are scattered

rough surface

Reflection of light rays

normal – a line drawn at right angles to a mirror to help measure the angles.

incoming (incident) ray

angle of incidence

reflected ray

angle of reflection

mirror

The image appears to come from here.

Practice

3 What does 'non-luminous' mean?

4 Why can't you see your reflection in a wooden desk top?

5 If the angle of incidence of a ray on a mirror is 34°, what is the angle of reflection?

6 **Opaque** substances don't let light through. What can happen to a ray of light that hits an opaque substance?

7 **Translucent** substances let a small amount of light through them. What can happen to a ray of light that hits a translucent substance?

FACT

Mirrors were put on the Moon by Neil Armstrong and Buzz Aldrin. They were used to reflect laser light beams shone from Earth, and this helped scientists work out how far away the Moon was more accurately.

P6: Colours of light

In this unit you will learn to answer these questions:

- Can light be bent?
- What is a spectrum?
- How can we change colour?

Get started

Find a glass or jar and half fill it with water. Stick a pen or pencil in the water and then look at it from the side. Draw what you see.

If you look at something on the bottom of a swimming pool it's not in the place that you think it is because light changes direction as it goes from water into air. This is called **refraction**.

Write two lists of bullet points; one about reflection and one about refraction. Put your lists where you will find them tomorrow. When you find your lists, make sure they still make sense.

Refraction happens because light travels more slowly through dense things like glass and faster through less dense things like air. It travels fastest in empty space (a **vacuum**).

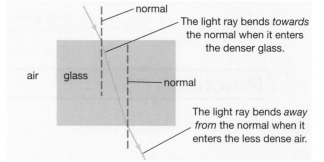

The light ray changes direction as it enters the air – it refracts.

Light from the object *appears* to be coming from here.

When light enters a more dense substance, it slows down and bends 'towards the normal'. The opposite happens when it enters a less dense substance.

air   glass

normal

The light ray bends *towards* the normal when it enters the denser glass.

normal

The light ray bends *away from* the normal when it enters the less dense air.

Practice

1 What is refraction?

2 In which of these will light travel fastest?

brick   glass   hydrogen gas   outer space

3 A light ray comes out of some clear plastic and into a gas. How does it change direction? Use the word 'normal' in your answer.

White light is made of different colours. Using a prism, you can make light bend twice. Some colours bend more than others and so the different colours separate out forming a **spectrum**. This is called **dispersion**.

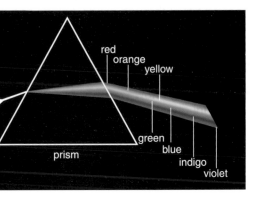

The colours of the spectrum

All the different colours of light can be made by combining the three **primary colours** (red, green and blue) in different amounts.

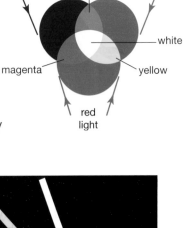

Coloured filters absorb some colours and let others through. Objects appear to be certain colours because of the colours of light that they absorb and reflect. White objects reflect all the colours. Black objects absorb all the colours.

The filter absorbs red and green light but allows blue light through.

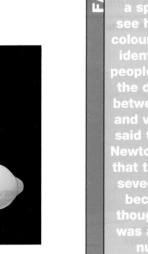

The lemon absorbs blue light but reflects red and green which together make yellow.

Practice

4 What is the splitting of light into the colours of the spectrum called?

5 What colour do blue and red lights combine to give?

6 Why does white light go green when it goes through a green filter?

7 A man is wearing white shorts, a blue T-shirt and a red cap. What colour will these look in the following colours of light. Draw a table for your answer. (*Hint:* Remember that blue objects reflect blue light but absorb green and red.)

a white light   b blue light   c red light

d green light   e magenta light

P9: Electrical circuits

Get started

Draw a diagram showing an electrical cell connected to a bulb, so that the bulb lights.

FACT Electricity travels around a circuit at 300 000 km/s (over 1 *billion* kilometres per hour).

In a circuit, energy is stored in the cell and is transferred by electricity to the **bulb**. Light waves are produced in a bulb, which transfer energy out of a circuit. Electricity only flows if there are no gaps in a circuit. A circuit without gaps is a **complete circuit**. A **switch** can make or close a gap in a circuit to turn **components** on and off.

We use circuit diagrams to show circuits, with **symbols** for the components.

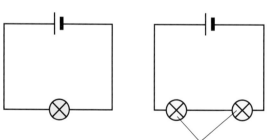

+ – cell (a cell has a positive (+) end and a negative (–) end)

——— connecting wire

—⊗— lamp (bulb)

—ᵒ⁄ ᵒ— switch (open)

—ᵒ—ᵒ— switch (closed)

Invent silly ways to remember which way round things go. For example, the longer line of the cell symbol is '+' because a '+' sign has a longer total length of line in it than a '–' sign!

If more than one bulb is connected to a cell, both bulbs will be less bright. Bulbs connected one after the other are said to be connected in **series**.

bulbs less bright

Practice

1 Name one component of a circuit.

2 Why won't the bulb in the top diagram light up?

3 a Draw a diagram of a circuit with three bulbs in series and one cell.

  b How bright will these bulbs be compared with a circuit with two bulbs and one cell?

Flowing electricity is called a **current**. A current is measured by connecting an **ammeter** in series with other components.

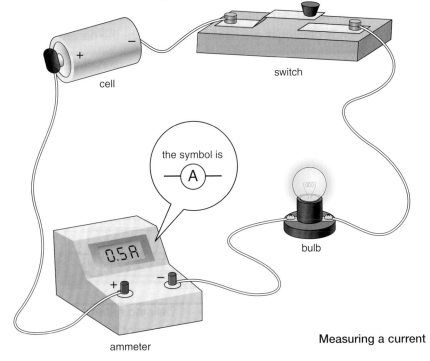

the symbol is
— (A) —

Measuring a current

Ammeters measure current in **amps** (**A**). The current is the same all the way around a circuit – it does *not* get used up.

Bulbs create **resistance** in a circuit. Resistance slows the current down and so the more bulbs, the less the current in the whole circuit. The slower the current, the less bright the bulbs. Components called resistors can also reduce the current in a circuit.

A current is caused by a cell. The more **voltage** a cell has, the greater its 'pushing power' and the faster a current will flow. Voltage is measured in **volts** (**V**).

Lots of cells connected together make a **battery**. The drawings below show three batteries (the dotted line means 'lots of cells').

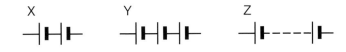

X   Y   Z

Use a **model** to think about things that you can't see. To think about electricity, imagine a river of hot water. The heat is like the electrical energy. The flow of water is like the current. The water carries the heat, which is lost as the water cools. The water itself is not used up and so the current doesn't get used up. An electrical current loses the electrical energy it's carrying to bulbs in a circuit, but this does not slow it down. However, this model can't be used to think about resistance. A better model (using a central heating system) is in the next unit.

FACT

Amps and volts are named after famous scientists who studied electricity – André Marie Ampère (1775–1836) and Alessandro Volta (1745–1827)

Practice

4 Draw a circuit diagram for the circuit at the top of the page.

5 Three cells have voltages 1.5 V, 6 V and 9 V. Which will produce the biggest current in a circuit?

6 Look at the symbols shown above for the batteries X, Y and Z.

  a Make up a rule for how cells should be connected to make a battery.

  b How many cells are there in batteries X, Y and Z?

Get started

In this unit you will learn to answer these questions:

▶ What are we paying for when we use electricity?
▶ Where do we get electricity from?
▶ How can we reduce the wastage of energy?

Put these appliances in order according to how much energy they use, starting with the least energy-consuming one.

electric clock   light bulb   stereo   television   toaster   tumble dryer

We use **mains electricity** in our homes, supplied at 230 V. Appliances that plug into the mains supply transform electrical energy into other types of energy. For example a toaster transforms electrical energy into heat energy.

The energy we use from the mains needs to be paid for and every house has an electricity meter that records the amount of energy used. Appliances often show a **power rating**, which is the number of **joules (J)** of electricity used in a second. The rating is given in **watts (W)** (1 W = 1 J used per second).

Appliance	Power (W)	Daily use (hours)	Cost per year (£)
18 W energy-saving light bulb	18	4	3
100 W light bulb	100	4	15
computer	250	2	18
television	290	4	42
vacuum cleaner	630	0.5	3
washing machine	930	1.5	8
electric oven	1800	1	66
electric kettle	2200	0.2	13

Electricity is generated in power stations. These often burn fossil fuels to change water into steam, which is used to turn a generator to produce electricity.

FACT There are 14 coal-fired power stations in the UK, burning about 33 million tonnes of coal each year.

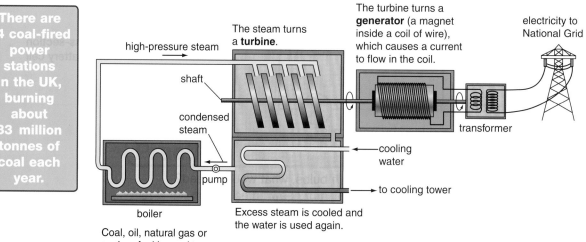

high-pressure steam

The steam turns a **turbine**.

The turbine turns a **generator** (a magnet inside a coil of wire), which causes a current to flow in the coil.

electricity to National Grid

shaft

condensed steam

transformer

cooling water

to cooling tower

pump

boiler

Excess steam is cooled and the water is used again.

Coal, oil, natural gas or nuclear fuel is used to heat water to turn it into steam.

What happens inside a power station

Practice

1 Draw an energy flow diagram for the power station. Start with chemical energy in coal.

2 What is the power rating of an average washing machine?

3 How many joules of energy does an average computer use each second?

The UK generates 50 million tonnes of carbon dioxide each year by burning fossil fuels in power stations. Carbon dioxide is a **greenhouse gas** (see page 103). Burning coal produces the most carbon dioxide; burning natural gas the least.

Renewable energy resources (e.g. wind, hydroelectricity) don't produce carbon dioxide but they cause other problems. For instance, wind farms are noisy and spoil the landscape, and hydroelectric power stations destroy habitats.

A coal-fired power station has an **efficiency** of 36%. This means that only 36% of the useful chemical energy stored in the coal is transformed into electrical energy. The rest is **wasted energy** (mainly heat energy). Household appliances also have efficiency ratings. A light bulb is only about 20% efficient but an energy-saving bulb giving the same amount of light is about 80% efficient.

Energy changes can be shown in diagrams like this:

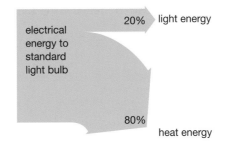

electrical energy to standard light bulb — 20% light energy — 80% heat energy

'Energy cannot be created or destroyed, only transformed from one form into another.' This is the **law of conservation of energy**. Try to learn it by heart.

FACT The muscles in your body are about 25% efficient.

Practice

4 Why does carbon dioxide cause problems?

5 What is wasted energy?

6 Draw a table to show the useful and wasted energies from these appliances: car, hair dryer, television, torch.

7 What is the efficiency of a coal-fired power station?

8 a Draw a diagram, like the one above, for an energy-saving light bulb.

b If you put your hand near both an energy-saving bulb and a normal light bulb, what difference would you expect to feel?

c Why would you expect to feel this difference?

d If 100 J of electrical energy go into an energy-saving light bulb, how many joules of light energy does it produce?

e Why is using energy-saving light bulbs a good idea?

9 A car is 25% efficient. For every 50 J of chemical energy in the petrol, how much useful kinetic energy does it produce?

P13: Different forces

In this unit you will learn to answer these questions:

▶ What are contact and non-contact forces?

▶ Why do things float?

▶ How do different materials stretch?

Get started

Draw a diagram of yourself pushing a wheelbarrow and label the forces. (Think about the weight of the wheelbarrow, the strain force of your arms and your pushing force.)

Every force:

● is either a push or a pull

● has a certain size

● has a certain direction

● can change something's shape, and/or its speed, and/or its direction.

Contact forces need to touch things. **Friction** is a contact force that pulls back on things rubbing against each other. **Drag** is the friction caused by things moving through air or water (**air resistance** and **water resistance**). **Upthrust** pushes up on things that are in water. There are many other contact forces, like the force from your chair pushing up on you.

Non-contact forces include **static electricity**, **magnetism** and **gravity**.

A forcemeter is used to measure the force of gravity on something.

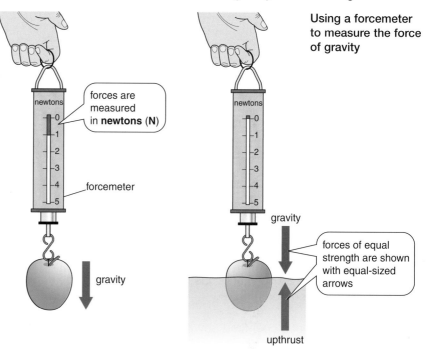

Using a forcemeter to measure the force of gravity

forces are measured in **newtons (N)**

forcemeter

gravity

gravity

forces of equal strength are shown with equal-sized arrows

upthrust

FACT

The dimples on a golf ball are designed to reduce the effect of air resistance and so allow the ball to fly further through the air.

The force of gravity is lessened by forces like upthrust. When something floats the forces of gravity and upthrust are the same but in opposite directions – they are **balanced forces**.

Practice

1 a What is drag?   b Name two types of drag.

2 a What is a non-contact force?   b Name three non-contact forces.

Inside a forcemeter is a spring. When the apple is put on the forcemeter, the force of gravity causes the spring to stretch. After it has stretched a certain distance there is enough **strain force** in the spring to balance the force of gravity and so the spring stops getting longer.

In an investigation different weights were added to a spring and the amount that it stretched was measured. The graph below shows the results.

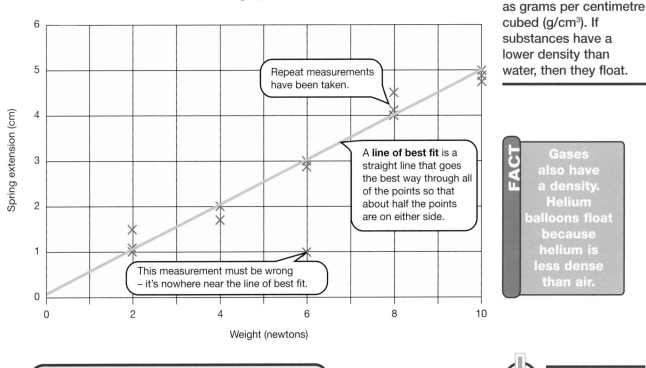

Practice

3 Copy the diagram of the forcemeter holding up the apple in the air. Add in another force arrow to show the force that balances the weight of the apple.

4 What are balanced forces?

5 Look at the graph above showing the spring extension for various weights.

a Why is it a good idea to take repeat measurements?

b What does the graph tell you? Try to come up with a rule for what happens when you add more weight to the spring.

P14: Weight and friction

In this unit you will learn to answer these questions:
- What is weight?
- What does friction do?
- What affects how quickly a car stops?

Get started

How much do you think a bag of six apples weighs? Have a guess.

A bag of six apples has a **mass** of about 600 g. It has a **weight** of about 6 newtons (6 N). Weight is the *force* with which gravity pulls on something and so it is measured in newtons. Mass is a measure of how much matter something contains. Every 1 kg mass has a weight of about 10 N on Earth.

When a wooden block is dragged across a surface, friction pulls back on the block. The amount of friction can be measured using a forcemeter.

Investigation to measure the amount of friction when pulling a wooden block

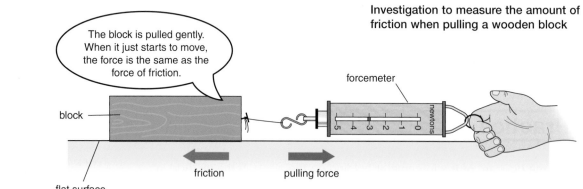

The block is pulled gently. When it just starts to move, the force is the same as the force of friction.

block

forcemeter

friction

pulling force

flat surface

⚠️ Write bulleted lists of ways to increase or decrease friction.

If more weight is added to the block the friction will be increased. The friction will also be increased by making the surface rougher or by increasing the area of the block in contact with the surface. Friction can be reduced by liquids (e.g. water, oil) between the surfaces. These liquids are called **lubricants**.

Practice

1
a A packet of sugar has a mass of 1 kg. What does it weigh?

b A potato has a mass of 500 g. What does it weigh?

c A melon weighs 20 N. What is its mass?

2 What is lubrication?

3 A wooden block was pulled across different surfaces. Rough sandpaper required 20 N of force to get the block to move, and fine sandpaper required 12 N of force.

a What force do you predict would be needed for medium sandpaper?

b What factors would need to be kept the same to make this a fair test?

Friction can be a problem. The metal parts of an engine get hot and wear away because of friction. Oil is used as a lubricant to stop this happening. Fast cars have **streamlined** shapes so that air can flow across them easily, reducing air resistance.

However, friction is also useful in cars. Friction between the tyres and the road surface allows a car to move and stop without slipping and sliding. The brakes also use friction.

The diagram below shows the **stopping distances** of a car on a dry road. A stopping distance is made up of the **thinking distance** and the **braking distance**.

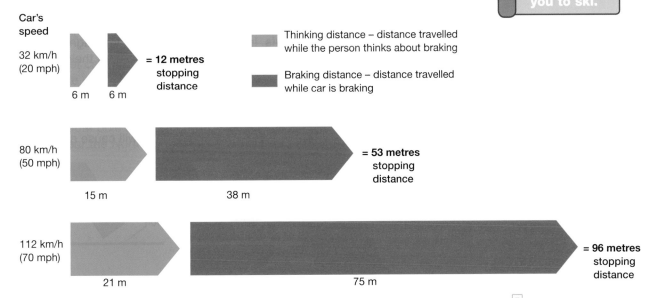

Car's speed

32 km/h (20 mph) = **12 metres** stopping distance

6 m   6 m

Thinking distance – distance travelled while the person thinks about braking

Braking distance – distance travelled while car is braking

80 km/h (50 mph) = **53 metres** stopping distance

15 m   38 m

112 km/h (70 mph) = **96 metres** stopping distance

21 m   75 m

You can see from the diagram that the faster the speed, the longer it takes to stop. Cars take longer to stop in the rain because the water on the road acts as a lubricant.

Have a go at drawing a concept map for the information on the last four pages. If you don't know what a concept map is, have a look at page 6. Use the diagram below to get started:

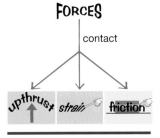

FORCES

contact

upthrust   strain   friction

Practice

4 a What is the stopping distance of a car going at 20 mph?

b What does 'mph' stand for?

5 Why should cars travel more slowly when it is raining?

6 Why do cars skid when they brake on ice?

7 Explain why friction is useful when you walk.

8 Think up one other way in which friction is useful and one other way in which it's not.

P16: Electromagnets

In this unit you will learn to answer these questions:

In this unit you will learn to answer these questions:

▶ How can electricity make a magnet?

▶ How can we explain how electromagnets work?

Get started

What is an electromagnet? Choose the best of these answers:

● A magnet made by the Electro Company.

● A magnet made using electricity.

● Something that is only a magnet when electricity flows through it.

● A magnet made of electrons.

FACT

The electro-magnet was invented in 1820 by D. F. Arago.

Passing an electric current through a coil of wire will make an **electromagnet**. An investigation was done to see how the strength of an electromagnet can be changed.

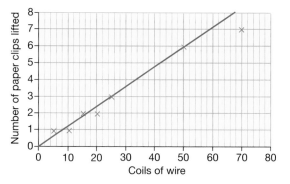

Here are the results:

Graph to show strength of electromagnet with changing voltage

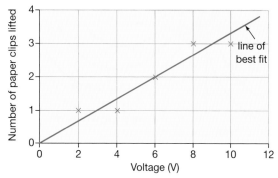

Graph to show strength of electromagnet with changing number of coils

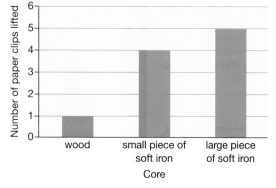

Graph to show strength of electromagnet with changing core

Practice

❶ How can the strength of the electromagnet be increased?

The diagram shows a doorbell. When you press the button, the circuit is closed and current flows. This makes the coil of wire into an electromagnet, which attracts the iron piston and this slides to the right. It hits the 'tone bar' and makes a note. When you take your finger off the button, the spring pulls the piston back into place, hitting the other tone bar and making another note. So you end up with 'bing-bong'.

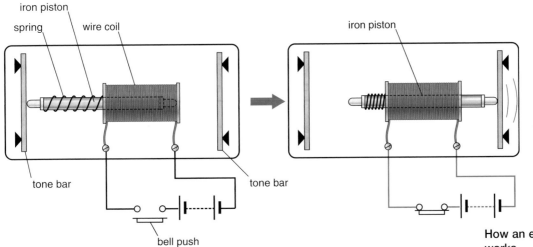

How an electric doorbell works

The magnetic field around an electromagnet is the same shape as the field around a bar magnet.

Practice

2 a Look at the investigation on the facing page. When changing the number of coils, what factors (or variables) must be kept the same to make this a fair test?

b The result for 70 coils of wire in the investigation is probably wrong. Suggest some reasons why it might be wrong.

c Reliable results are ones that you can be sure of. How could the results be made more reliable?

d How could you improve the investigation to get more detailed (accurate) readings?

3 When the button of the doorbell described above is pushed, what happens just outside the coil of wire?

4 a Which end of the electromagnet in the diagram on the right is north?

b How did you work out your answer?

Design a concept map using these words to start you off:

magnet magnetic field north south attract repel electromagnet

FACT Electro-magnets are also used in loudspeakers (see page 116), electric motors and Maglev trains (which float above their tracks owing to forces of repulsion).

P20: Pressure

Get started

Why is it more comfortable to lie on a hard floor than on a bed of nails?

Remember how to calculate pressure using this triangle – cover up the P and it shows that you need to divide force by area. Think up a mnemonic to remember the order of letters (e.g. Football Playing Area).

Pressure is the amount of force on a certain area. Its units are N/cm² or N/m² or **pascals (Pa)**. 1 Pa = 1 N/m².

weight = 720 N

area of both shoes = 180 cm²

To find the pressure you divide the force by the area. For example:

force = 720 N   area = 180 cm²

pressure of shoes = $\frac{720}{180}$ = 4 N/cm²

Pressure can be lowered by increasing the area over which the force acts. Snowshoes have a larger area than normal shoes to stop you sinking into the snow.

Pressure can be raised by decreasing the area over which the force acts. Knives have blades with a small area to increase the pressure so that they cut better. Nails have sharp points so they can be hammered in more easily.

FACT
The pascal is named after a French mathematician called Blaise Pascal (1623–1662) who did important experiments in measuring air pressure.

Practice

1 What is pressure?

2 Work out these pressures:

a a force of 10 N on an area of 2 cm²

b a force of 25 N on an area of 5 m²

3 Camels live in sandy deserts. Why do they have big feet?

The particles in a gas are far apart, so a gas can be **compressed** (squashed). **Pneumatic** tyres have air under pressure inside them. These support the weight of the vehicle but can squash to even out bumps in the road.

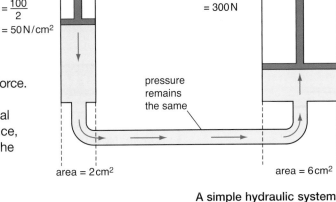

force = 100 N

$P = \dfrac{F}{A}$

$= \dfrac{100}{2}$

$= 50 \,\text{N/cm}^2$

upwards force:
$F = P \times A$
$= 50 \times 6$
$= 300 \,\text{N}$

Liquids cannot be compressed and so can be used in **hydraulic** systems to carry a force from one place to another and to change the size of the force.

Hydraulics are used in car brakes. The brake pedal moves a disc with a small diameter a large distance, and this action is used to move large discs near the wheels a small distance.

pressure remains the same

area = 2 cm²

area = 6 cm²

A simple hydraulic system

Gases and liquids have an **internal pressure**, which means that something put in them will feel a pressure on it. If you dive underwater you can feel this pressure on your ears.

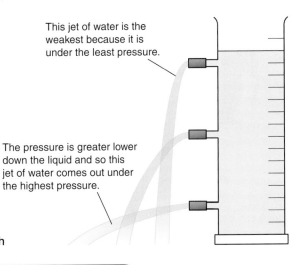

This jet of water is the weakest because it is under the least pressure.

The pressure is greater lower down the liquid and so this jet of water comes out under the highest pressure.

How pressure varies with depth

FACT Pneumatic tyres were invented twice. Robert Thompson invented them in 1845 but no one paid much attention. A Scottish vet called John Dunlop reinvented them, making three tyres to fit on his young son's tricycle, in 1888.

Practice

4 Look at the diagram of the hydraulic system above. A force of 250 N is applied to the cylinder on the left.

  a What pressure will it exert on the liquid?

  b What will be the pressure on the right-hand cylinder?

  c What force will push up on the right-hand cylinder?

  d Which will move the greater distance, the left- or the right-hand cylinder?

5 Why won't a car's braking system work very well if air gets into it?

6 In the diagram of the cylinder of water above, why is the jet of water at the bottom stronger than the one at the top?

7 A table tennis ball is taken down to the ocean floor by a diver. The ball crumples on its way down. Why?

8 A party balloon is taken to the top of Mount Everest. It is bigger at the top of the mountain than at the bottom. Why is this?

9 Dams are used to hold back large volumes of water in reservoirs. Why are dam walls thicker at the bottom than at the top?

In this unit you will learn to answer these questions:

▶ How do levers work?

▶ How do things balance?

Get started

Find a door and gently push it open by putting your hand next to the handle. Now try to push the door open with your hand next to the hinges. Which was easier? Why do you think door handles are placed well away from the hinges?

Something that can change the direction or the size of a force is called a **machine**. A **lever** is a simple machine that uses a **pivot** (or **fulcrum**).

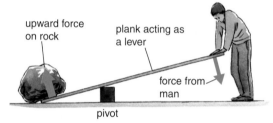

upward force on rock

plank acting as a lever

force from man

pivot

In the diagram on the left, the force of the man pushing down is not in the same place as the force pushing up from the pivot, so the lever turns. The force from the man causes a **turning effect** or **moment**.

A moment is measured in **newton metres (N m)** and is calculated by multiplying the force by the perpendicular distance from the pivot (perpendicular means at right angles to). The longer a lever, the easier it is to move things with it.

moment on right = 2 × 60
= 120 N m

force delivered to rock = $\dfrac{\text{moment}}{\text{distance}}$

= $\dfrac{120}{1}$ = 120 N

moment on right = 1 × 60
= 60 N m

force delivered to rock = $\dfrac{\text{moment}}{\text{distance}}$

= $\dfrac{60}{1}$ = 60 N

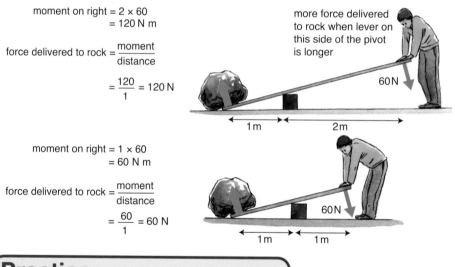

more force delivered to rock when lever on this side of the pivot is longer

60 N

1 m   2 m

60 N

1 m   1 m

Practice

1 What is a moment?

2 A woman opens a tin of paint with a screwdriver. She presses down on the handle 20 cm away from the pivot (the edge of the tin) with a force of 70 N.

a What is the moment? (Careful: Work in metres!)

b The end of the screwdriver under the lid is 1 cm from the pivot. What is the upward force on the lid?

3 a Sketch a pair of scissors and label the pivot.

b Why is it easier to cut things that are closer to the pivot?

Your lower arm bones are moved by an **antagonistic pair** of muscles (see page 31) and act as a lever with your elbow as the pivot. Bottle openers, scissors and spanners are all further examples of levers.

If a force acts on one side of a see-saw, that side sinks due to the moment of the force. If a force is applied to the other side, there will be two moments in opposite directions. If the moments are the same, the see-saw will balance.

This same idea is used in tower cranes, where a block of concrete (the counterweight) balances the weight of the load being lifted.

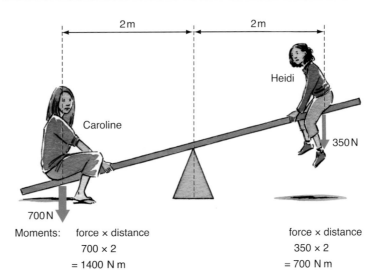

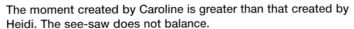

Moments: force × distance   force × distance
               700 × 2   350 × 2
               = 1400 N m   = 700 N m

The moment created by Caroline is greater than that created by Heidi. The see-saw does not balance.

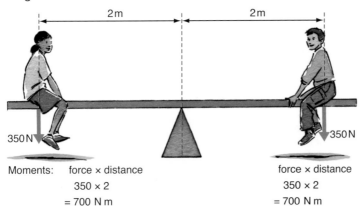

Moments: force × distance   force × distance
               350 × 2   350 × 2
               = 700 N m   = 700 N m

The two moments are equal. The see-saw balances.

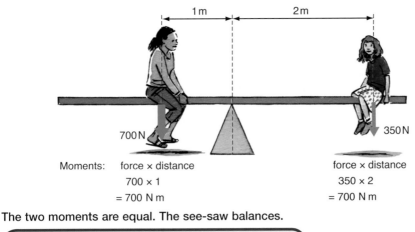

Moments: force × distance   force × distance
               700 × 1   350 × 2
               = 700 N m   = 700 N m

The two moments are equal. The see-saw balances.

FACT

Leonardo da Vinci (1452–1519) cut up human bodies and used pieces of string to replace muscles. He would pull the strings to see how the bones operated as levers.

Practice

④ Work out the moments for the following pairs of people who are sitting opposite each other on see-saws. Say whether each see-saw will balance:

a Chantelle weighs 500 N and sits 1.5 m from the pivot. Anna weighs 500 N and sits 1.5 m from the pivot on the other side.

b Dave weighs 450 N and sits 2 m from the pivot. Michael weighs 300 N and sits 3 m from the pivot on the other side.

c Taylor has a mass of 60 kg and sits 150 cm from the pivot. Courtney has a mass of 40 kg and sits 2 m from the pivot on the other side.

Use all the words in bold on pages 142–145 to make a concept map.

P22: Sun, Moon and Earth

In this unit you will learn to answer these questions:
- ▶ Why do we have days, months and years?
- ▶ How do we see the Sun and Moon?

Get started

Why does the Moon shine? Draw a diagram for your answer.

The Earth's orbit

Look at the letters on the diagram below and read the information about them.

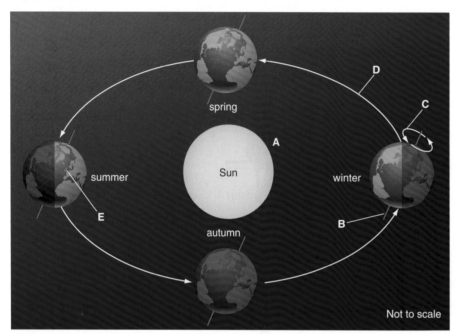

A You can see the Sun because light travels from the **Sun** to the **Earth**.

B The **axis** is an imaginary line that goes from pole to pole. The Earth has two **hemispheres** and each has a **pole** (the **North pole** and the **South pole**).

C The Earth takes 24 hours to spin once around its axis. As it spins parts of the Earth get lit by the Sun and then hidden from the Sun, giving **day** and **night**. As this happens, it seems to us that the Sun moves across the sky.

D The Earth *also* travels around the Sun in an **orbit**. It takes $365\frac{1}{4}$ days to complete one orbit. (365 days is 1 **year**). Every 4 years the four quarter days are added up to give us an extra day in February. This is a **leap year**.

E The Earth's axis is tilted which gives us **seasons**. In summer the **Northern hemisphere** points towards the Sun and so spends more time in sunlight. Days are longer in summer and so it is hotter. When it's summer in the UK it's winter in the **Southern hemisphere**.

FACT The Arctic Circle is the area of the Northern hemisphere where, on one or more days each year, the Sun never rises.

Practice

1 Rewrite paragraph E to talk about what happens in winter.

2 What is:

a an orbit

b the axis of the Earth

c a hemisphere of the Earth?

The Sun makes its own light and so is a **luminous source**. The **Moon** does not make its own light – it is a **non-luminous source**. However you can see the Moon because it **reflects** light from the Sun.

The Moon takes 28 days to orbit the Earth – a **lunar month**. As it travels around the Earth people on Earth can see less or more of its lit side and it looks as if the Moon changes shape. This is called the **phases of the Moon**.

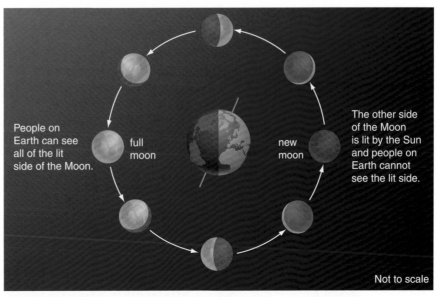

People on Earth can see all of the lit side of the Moon.

full moon

new moon

The other side of the Moon is lit by the Sun and people on Earth cannot see the lit side.

Not to scale

Sometimes the Moon gets between the Sun and the Earth. Its shadow falls on the Earth causing a **solar eclipse** (the sunlight is blocked and it goes dark).

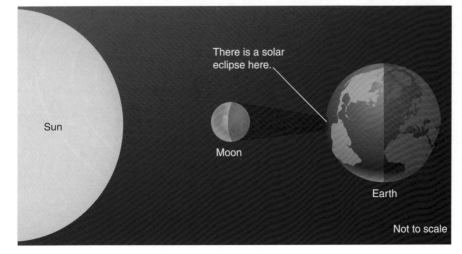

Sun

There is a solar eclipse here.

Moon

Earth

Not to scale

Write a list of all the words in bold on these two pages. Then go through them one at a time, making sure you can say what each one means.

A **lunar eclipse** is when the Earth's shadow falls on the Moon.

Practice

3 a Why is it easy to see a full moon?

b Why is it hard to see a new moon?

c Draw out what the nine phases of the Moon look like from Earth, starting and ending with a new moon.

4 Street lights come on automatically at night time when it goes dark. Why do they come on during a solar eclipse?

5 Draw a diagram of a lunar eclipse. Remember the Earth is bigger than the Moon.

FACT The last total solar eclipse visible from the UK was in 1999.

P23: The Solar System

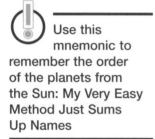

Use this mnemonic to remember the order of the planets from the Sun: My Very Easy Method Just Sums Up Names

Get started

Shut the book and write down as many words to do with the Solar System as you can think of.

The **Solar System** contains a **star** (the Sun), eight planets and a band of large rocks called the **asteroid belt**. There are also two dwarf planets, Pluto and Ceres (which is in the asteroid belt). The **asteroids** and the planets orbit the Sun.

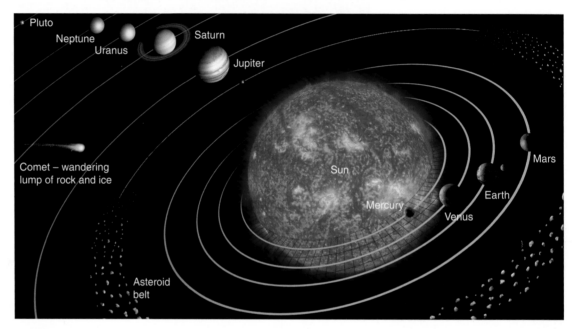

Scientists find out about the Solar System by using **telescopes** or sending out **space probes** that send information back to Earth. The table shows some of the things we know about the other planets.

FACT There are over 100 000 other large (bigger than 50 km across) rocky objects beyond the orbit of Neptune in a region called the Kuiper belt. Pluto is in this belt.

Planet	Time for 1 rotation	Time for 1 orbit	Distance from Sun (million km)	Mean surface temperature (°C)
Mercury	59 days	88 Earth days	58	170
Venus	243 days	224 Earth days	108	460
Earth	24 hours	365 Earth days	150	15
Mars	25 hours	687 Earth days	228	−50
Jupiter	10 hours	12 Earth years	778	−143
Saturn	10 hours	30 Earth years	1427	−195
Uranus	17 hours	84 Earth years	2871	−201
Neptune	16 hours	165 Earth years	4497	−220

1 Which planet has a day length most similar to Earth's?

2 How long does it take for Neptune to go once around the Sun?

3 a What do you notice about the temperatures of the planets as they get further from the Sun?

 b Why do you think this is?

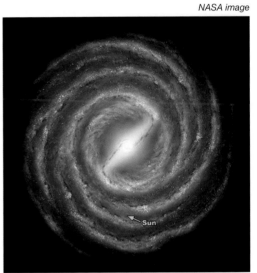

NASA image

Scientists think that for life to exist there must be liquid water, oxygen and a temperature that is not too hot or cold. Earth is the only place in the Solar System that has these conditions.

Outside the Solar System is the rest of the **Universe**. It contains billions of other stars that exist in huge clumps called **galaxies**. Our Sun is in a galaxy called the **Milky Way**.

Although stars are luminous sources, we can't see them during the day because the light from the Sun is so bright. We can see them at night though. Through history people have joined the stars with imaginary lines to form objects. Groups of stars linked in this way are called **constellations**.

The Milky Way

Just as the Sun appears to move across the daytime sky as the Earth turns, so the stars appear to move across the night-time sky as the Earth turns.

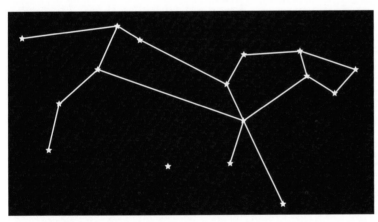

The constellation of Leo (a lion)

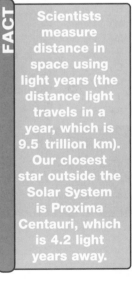

FACT Scientists measure distance in space using light years (the distance light travels in a year, which is 9.5 trillion km). Our closest star outside the Solar System is Proxima Centauri, which is 4.2 light years away.

Practice

4 What is the Milky Way?

5 Why do we think that Earth is the only place in the Solar System with life?

6 Why do constellations appear to move across the sky at night?

7 Think up four multiple-choice questions using the information on the last four pages. Try out your questions on someone else!

P24: Space

In this unit you will learn to answer these questions:

▶ How have our ideas about the Solar System changed?

▶ What keeps the planets and satellites in orbit?

Get started

Sketch a diagram of the Solar System and label the planets.

The Ancient Babylonians (about 10 000 years ago) thought that the Earth was a mountain standing in a huge, flat sea with a solid dome of sky above.

About 2350 years ago, the Greek thinker Aristotle said that the Earth was a sphere and that the planets, Moon and Sun were stuck to see-through spheres that rotated around the Earth.

This was followed by the modern idea of planets, but with the Earth still at the centre of the Solar System (a geocentric model). However, a good theory allows you to make predictions, and predictions about where the planets should be on a certain day didn't work using a simple geocentric model. Extra circles were added to the orbits to try to make predictions about the positions of the planets more accurate. It all got very complicated!

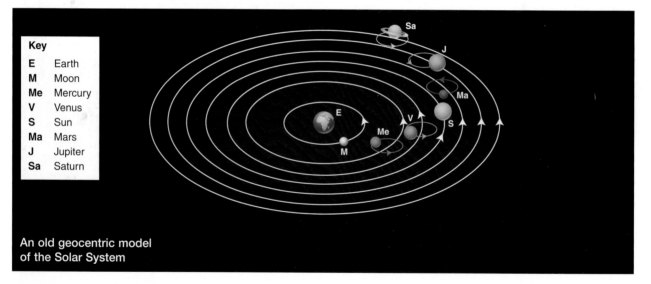

Key

E	Earth
M	Moon
Me	Mercury
V	Venus
S	Sun
Ma	Mars
J	Jupiter
Sa	Saturn

An old geocentric model of the Solar System

Nicolaus Copernicus (1473–1543) suggested that the planets went around the Sun. Johannes Kepler (1571–1630) refined Copernicus's theory by giving the planets oval (elliptical) orbits, not circular ones. We still use Kepler's theory since it explains all the evidence and allows us to make accurate predictions.

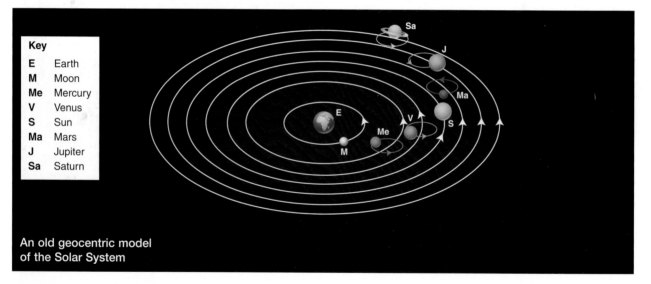

FACT
About 2900 years ago the Indian thinker Yajnavalkya first suggested that the planets went around the Sun!

Practice

1 What current evidence tells us that the Ancient Babylonian idea is wrong?

2 What should a good theory be able to do?

3 How was Kepler's idea different from Copernicus's?

The gravitational pull of the Sun keeps the planets in their orbits. The gravitational pull of the Earth keeps the Moon orbiting around it. The Moon is a **natural satellite** of the Earth. Other planets have moons too – there are thought to be about 160 moons in the Solar System.

Artificial satellites are used for many things, including recording weather patterns, transmitting TV pictures and phone calls, making maps and spying. Some artificial satellites remain above the same part of the Earth all the time and go around the Earth at the same speed as the Earth is rotating. They are said to be in **geostationary orbits**.

Satellites in **polar orbits** move around the Earth from pole to pole while the Earth turns beneath them.

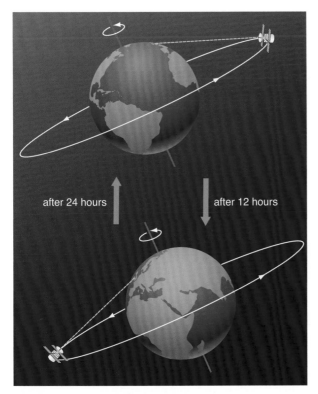

A satellite in a geostationary orbit

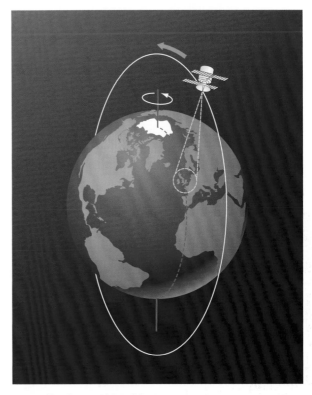

A satellite in a polar orbit

Some artificial satellites have been put into orbit around other planets to find out more about them.

Practice

4 What is the name of the Earth's natural satellite?

5 You have been asked to write a one-sentence definition of the word 'satellite' for a dictionary. What would you write?

6 What type of orbit do you think artificial satellites should have for the following:

   a TV transmission

   b mapping the Earth

   c transmitting phone signals?

Go through these two pages and the pages about 'Gravity' (pages 136–137). Write down six key points about gravity and space.

Answers

B1: Cells

Get started: The mains ones are: brain (controls the body), ear (hearing), eye (sight), gullet or foodpipe (taking food to stomach), heart (pumping blood), kidneys (cleaning the blood), large intestine (removes water from food), liver (making and destroying substances), lungs (breathing), skin (protection and feeling), small intestine (digesting food), stomach (digesting food), windpipe or trachea (taking air to and from lungs).

1 Check your list with the Glossary.
2 ×200
3 keeps a specimen flat and stops it drying out on a slide
4 your own answer
5 controls a cell's activities
6 supports and protects a plant cell
7 cytoplasm, nucleus, cell surface membrane
8 **a** See the diagram at the top of page 9.
   b Plant cell, because it has a cell wall, a vacuole and chloroplasts.
9 Chloroplast, because all the others are found in both plants and animals (there are other correct answers!).
10 your own drawing with cytoplasm, cell surface membrane and nucleus labelled

B2: Tissues and organs

Get started: A neurone, B sperm cell, C ciliated epithelial cell

1 a group of cells of the same type
2 root
3 number of cells increases by cell division and cells get bigger
4 they are long to carry information a long way
5 **a** 300 grams of sugar per litre; **b** number of pollen tubes that grew in different sugar solutions (or something along those lines!); **c** so you can be sure that a result is right
6 **a** like one of the cells in the diagram on page 10 with labels; **b** It has a 'root hair' that provides more surface area for water to get into the cell.
7 ciliated epithelial tissue
8 diagram of cell division like the one on page 10

B3: The reproductive system

Get started: Something like this:

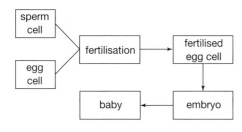

1 Ducks use internal fertilisation and goldfish use external fertilisation. Internal fertilisation is more likely to result in fertilised egg cells and ducks look after their young, so they need to produce fewer offspring to ensure that some survive.
2 uterus
3 **a** 3; **b** 28 October; **c** uterus lining passes out of vagina; **d** to make sure that if an embryo is formed it has a fresh lining
4 testes
5 **a** uterus – where the embryo/fetus/baby develops; **b** sperm duct – carries sperm cells from the testes to the urethra; **c** oviduct – carries egg cells from the ovary to the uterus

B4: Growth and development

Get started: Something like this:

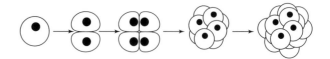

1 Milk provides all the nutrients it needs to grow.
2 the uterus contracts
3 your own list
4 your own list
5 lungs → blood → placenta → umbilical cord → fetus's blood → fetus's brain
6 **a** chemicals made by the body that travel in the blood; **b** cause changes in the body
7 The sample size is too small.

B5: The digestive system

Get started: Mouth, gullet, stomach, small intestine, large intestine, rectum, anus – the order of organs that your food travels through.

1 Food is digested and absorbed.
2 breaking down
3

Nutrient	Digested in...
starch	mouth, small intestine
sugars	small intestine
proteins	stomach, small intestine
fats	small intestine

4 **a** enzymes; **b** to break down food
5 carbohydrate, sugar
6 to create a large surface area to absorb digested food quickly

B6: Respiration and the circulatory system

Get started: All of them

1 **a** 7 °C; **b** that peas are respiring because heat is produced during respiration; **c** There would be no increase in temperature.

2   glucose, oxygen
3   Similarities – both use up oxygen, produce heat energy, produce carbon dioxide, produce water, need a fuel; differences – no flame in respiration, much less heat produced in respiration.
4   carbon dioxide, water (energy is not a substance and so is not a product)
5   It has two halves which each act as a pump, pumping blood to two different places.
6   small intestine → villus → blood vessels → liver → blood vessels → heart → blood vessels → leg muscle
7   lung → blood vessels → heart → blood vessels → leg muscle
8   Blood carries oxygen and glucose to cells which are needed for respiration, and blood carries away the carbon dioxide that cells produce when they respire.

B7: The breathing system

Get started: You should feel your chest push out on your hand; you should feel your chest rising out and up.
1   thin walls, covered in capillaries, large surface area
2   transferring oxygen into the blood and carbon dioxide out of the blood
3   Respiration is a chemical reaction; breathing is a movement of muscles; ventilation is a flowing of air.
4   a indicator turns yellow; b Carbon dioxide is produced by the respiring peas. c no colour change
5   Poor gas exchange since there is less surface area.

B8: Microbes and disease

Get started: Your own answer.
1   a temperature, size of measuring cylinder, type of bread dough, amount of bread dough, time dough was left for; b The yeast produces carbon dioxide as it respires. c The more glucose, the more the bread rises. d glucose; e The dough would not rise.
2   a making cheese and yoghurt (there are other uses); b 30 °C
3   Your poster should mention avoiding breathing in people's sneezes, maybe telling others to use a handkerchief; making sure that meats are cooked properly; making sure that water is safe to drink; not touching blisters and rashes on someone else; taking precautions (like using a condom) during sexual intercourse.
4   flu – caused by a virus (all the others are caused by different bacteria)

B9: Defence against diseases

Get started: Your own answer.
1   earwax in ears, lysozyme in tears, skin, hairs in nose, mucus in nose and windpipe, acid in stomach, ciliated epithelial cells in windpipe, scabs on skin (white blood cells are for when microbes get inside you, which wasn't the question!)
2   a chemical that destroys bacteria; b tears and sweat
3   protects the baby from diseases
4   Antibiotics only work against bacteria and flu is caused by a virus.
5   a an injection that contains a vaccine; b Vaccinations contain dead or weak microbes which the body makes antibodies against.
6   She doesn't have any antibodies against diphtheria and so it takes time for her body to start making antibodies against the microbe from scratch.

B10: Food and nutrition

Get started: The only true one is 'Fats are used for energy'.
1   Remember that water and fibre aren't nutrients.

Nutrient	Needed for...
proteins	growth and repair
carbohydrates	energy
fats	storing energy and heat insulation
minerals	keeping you healthy
vitamins	keeping you healthy

2   a 2 g, b to keep your gut healthy
3
- as a solvent
- for sweating
- to fill cells so they keep their shapes

4   a sugars, starch; b starch; c sugars; d starch – potatoes/bread/rice/pasta/cereals; sugars – any sweet things.
5   a add iodine solution; b You would expect the iodine solution to form a blue/black colour, showing that the potato contains starch.

6
Food substance	Examples of good source
proteins	two from: fish, meat, nuts, dairy products
carbohydrates	two from: bread, rice, pasta, potatoes, cereals
fats	two from: meat, dairy products, fish, nuts
vitamins	fruits, vegetables
minerals	two from: fruits, vegetables, fish, meat, nuts, dairy products
fibre	fruits, vegetables, cereals

7 carbohydrate (starch)
8 Your own poster; make sure it tells people what a balanced diet is.

B11: Fitness – smoking and diet

Get started: Your own answer.

1 a windpipe, heart, lungs, stomach, small intestine, large intestine, rectum, anus;
   b i – A, ii – C, iii – D, iv – B
2 We know more about the dangers of smoking now.
3 a Tar causes coughing. b The cilia stop working and can't clean the lungs.
4 for growth and repair
5 being very overweight
6 your own answer

B12: Fitness – drugs and exercise

Get started: Your own answer. Most people think it is a good idea because it prevents accidents.

1 brain, liver
2 The amount of time it takes you to do something in response to a situation.
3 It increases them.
4 Their bodies don't absorb vitamins and minerals so well.
5 oxygen and food (glucose)
6 your own answer
7 a biceps and triceps; b Muscles can only pull.
8 joins a muscle to a bone
9 a something that slows down the activity of your nerves; b Any one from: alcohol, heroin, marijuana.
10 stimulant, legal, drug, recreational drug
11 Examples: Do we live longer today than people of our great-grandparents' generation? Do we suffer from fewer diseases than people of our great-grandparents' generation?

B13: Habitats

Get started: your own list – most organisms that live underground are tube-shaped to allow them to move easily through tunnels.

1 Your own creation but it should be able to keep warm!
2 hot during the day and cold at night, dry
3 camouflage to avoid being spotted by predators
4 Arctic, desert, ocean, underground, wood
5 Daily changes happen every day, seasonal changes occur slowly over the course of a year.
6 a seasonal change; b It helps to keep it warm in winter.
7 There's not much food about in winter.
8 swallow – but there are plenty of other examples
9 an investigation where only one thing (called a factor or variable) is changed

B14: Feeding relationships

Get started: grass → rabbit → fox
– make sure you get the arrows the right way round. If you've got this wrong try remembering that the arrow means 'is eaten by'.

1 sharp claws for catching prey, forward-facing eyes for good, 3D vision, sharp teeth to rip apart flesh, runs fast
2 rose bush → aphid → ladybird
   producer   *consumer*   *consumer*
                 herbivore *carnivore*
                 prey   *predator*
3 Any of four food chains:
   bramble → wood mouse → stoat → fox
   or bramble → wood mouse → stoat → owl
   or grass → rabbit → stoat → fox
   or grass → rabbit → stoat → owl.
4 how the energy goes from organism to organism/what eats what
5 stoats, wood mice, bank voles and dormice
6
hedgehog ← ladybird
earthworm   aphid
dead leaves   rose bush

7 a Bank voles and dormice would have less to eat and some might starve. With fewer bank voles and dormice the owls would have to eat more wood mice and stoats and their populations might go down. b There would be less grass but the stoats and foxes would have more to eat and so more of them would survive. There are other answers to both parts a and b because all the organisms are connected together in a food web.
8 The stinging nettles sting their noses.

B15: More relationships

Get started: Foxes depend on rabbits for food and rabbits depend on grass:
grass → rabbit → fox

1 Their leaves wouldn't reach the surface and so wouldn't get enough light for photosynthesis.
2 streamlined shapes, way of holding onto rocks
3 big leaves
4 a lettuce → slug → thrush → sparrowhawk;

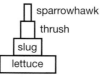
b

c the numbers of each type of organism as you go up a food chain; d As you go up a food chain there is less energy available and so there are fewer organisms.

5   There would be fewer thrushes (they would die of starvation or move out of the area to find spiders somewhere else) and more aphids (fewer spiders to eat them).

B16: Exploring habitats

Get started: Leaf shape, acorns, cones, shape of structure containing seeds

1   ferns, conifers, flowering plants
2   X = flowering plant, Y = conifer
3   They have no cuticle on their leaves and so lose water quickly.
4   a 1350; b ability to cope with salty water/ability to anchor in loose sand
5   fox, oak tree, rabbit, snail, wood pigeon
6   Different organisms have different adaptations for different conditions in different habitats.

B17: Photosynthesis

Get started: Light, water, carbon dioxide

1   a The graph shows that carbon dioxide levels vary over the day and are lowest near the middle of the day. b The Sun is brightest during the middle of the day and so this is when photosynthesis happens fastest and more carbon dioxide is used up.
2   They contain green chlorophyll/chloroplasts.
3   starch
4   a the green parts; b These parts contain the chlorophyll, so it is here that photosynthesis happens. The glucose made in photosynthesis is turned into starch. c chloroplasts
5   It goes up.
6   a aerobic respiration; b oxygen + glucose → carbon dioxide + water (+ energy)

B18: More photosynthesis

Get started: Your own answer, but your list may include things like food, paper, oils, fabrics (e.g. cotton), medicines, dyes.

1   Its leaves are not photosynthesising but its cells are respiring.
2   It needs nitrates to make proteins.
3   To make their plants grow better and produce more of the useful part of the crop (the yield).
4   You should have labelled the nucleus, cytoplasm, vacuole, cell surface membrane, cell wall, root hair.
5   They are spread out, branched, have root hair cells.
6   The cells in the roots can't get oxygen from the soil for aerobic respiration.
7   a tube that carries water in plants
8   They use up the carbon dioxide that animals produce and release oxygen.

9   a Burning produces carbon dioxide and fewer trees means that less carbon dioxide can be taken in for photosynthesis. b Plants and animals die out because their habitat is gone.
10 It would be too easy if you could just look up the answer here!

B19: Plants for food

Get started: Your own answer.

1   a oxygen, glucose; b carbon dioxide, water (note that energy is not a product because it is not a substance)
2   to make a store of energy
3   The trunk doesn't grow much.
4   the Sun
5   a nitrates, phosphates and compounds of potassium; b the soil
6   nitrogen
7   a the type of fertiliser; b the type of radish, soil, temperature, amount of water, number of radishes per pot; c probably between 5 and 10 (you need enough to be sure that your results show the correct pattern but not so many that it takes forever to do the investigation); d B; e It gave the highest growth. f mass, diameter, circumference or volume

B20: Growing plants

Get started: Fertiliser – to improve growth, slug pellets – to kill slugs, insecticide – to kill insect pests, fungicide – to kill fungi that cause disease, weedkiller – to kill weeds.

1   one that only kills certain plants
2   The yield of potato plants goes down if you leave the potato plants growing with weeds for too long.
3   Any three from: removing weeds, adding fertiliser, removing insects, keeping plants well watered.
4   There would be very few peacock butterflies.
5   an animal that damages crops
6   a Advantages – improves yields of crops; disadvantages – expensive, kills other animals and upsets the food web. b Advantages – improves yields, lets crops grow in areas they normally would not grow; disadvantages – looks ulgy, expensive.
7   weeds → snail → song thrush → sparrowhawk
8   a

```
            ┌──────────┐
            │  barn owl│
        ┌───┴──┬───────┘
        │ field│
        │ mouse│
    ┌───┴──────┴────┐
    │    wheat       │
    └────────────────┘
```

b field mouse; c Other animals that eat the weeds would die out.

B21: Variation

Get started: Tigers have stripes, lions don't; lions have tufted tails, tigers don't; tigers have white on their bellies, lions don't; tigers don't have manes, male lions do.

1 the differences between organisms
2 your own answers
3 **a** Do taller people have bigger hand widths? *or* Do smaller people have smaller hand widths? *or* Do taller people have smaller hand widths? *etc.* **b** Taller people have bigger hand widths.
4 no
5 Mum (blond) and Dad (straight)
6 It is a small type of plant, it is a young plant, it has not had enough fertiliser, it has not had enough light, it has not had enough water, someone has cut it back – there are plenty of reasons!
7 Eye colour is the only inherited characteristic (but you might have another answer which would be correct).
8 your own drawing

B22: Classification

Get started: Similarities – four limbs, hair, two eyes, body shape. Differences – bat has wings, bat has some limbs much longer than the others. When answering questions like this stick to things that you can see, because it's a much better way of classifying animals. Saying that bats fly is true but if you're trying to sort animals into groups of things that are most like each other you'll find that you end up putting bats with birds, when of course bats are mammals and not birds. The best way of telling these two animals apart is that bats have wings and hamsters don't.

1 **a** three body sections, six legs; **b** shape of antennae, pattern of stripes, colour of stripes
2 the largest groups that organisms are sorted into
3 body covering
4 on the basis of number of legs
5 animal kingdom, invertebrate, arthropod, insect
6 your own masterpiece!

B23: Inheritance

Get started: The dimple in his chin, eye colour or his ears, which don't have lobes.

1 animals – blue eyes, brown hair, dimpled chin, lobed ears, small nose;
plants – long roots, pink petals, spiky leaves

2 your own answer
3 It contains a complete set of genetic information (an egg cell only contains half the genetic information of a normal body cell).
4 **a** mass of apples; **b** Any one from: colour, volume, circumference, diameter. **c** ...variation within a variety. **d** using a balance that measures to more decimal places (accuracy is to do with how careful you are at measuring); **e** taking measurements from more apples (reliability is to do with how sure you can be that what your results show is actually true)
5 A bit of both – if your parents are tall you will be tall but if you don't eat enough food then you won't grow as tall.
6 physical environmental factors

B24: Selection

Get started: Your suggestions might include: good flavour, nice colour, fast growing, not affected by diseases, produce lots of strawberries.

1 Take two tall German shepherd dogs (a female and a male) and breed them. Then choose the tallest of the offspring and breed them with other tall German shepherds. If she does this over and over she will eventually end up with very tall German shepherds.
2 Any three from: lots of wool, high-quality wool, good meat, able to survive in harsh environment, produce lots of lambs.
3 breeding two varieties or breeds together
4 the amount of useful product you get from a plant or animal
5 You can see colour, amount of fruit; you can't see resistance to disease, taste, resistance to cold weather, lack of rotting.
6 sweet taste, large fruit, lots of fruit, resistance to disease, resistance to cold weather, resistance to rotting
7 to stop pollen from other plants pollinating the flower
8 **a** a ruler or a balance; **b** lots, say 20–30 of each type
9 The pollen grain and the egg cell only contain half the genetic information from parent plants and in this case they have contained the half which carried the features that Ravi didn't want.

C1: Acids and alkalis

Get started: Acids are sour to taste, can be dangerous, have pHs below 7; alkalis feel soapy to the touch, can be dangerous, have pHs above 7.

1 Hydrochloric acid and car battery acid, but you could also have things like sulfuric acid and nitric acid.
2 to dilute the acid so it is less dangerous
3 The real one looks like this:

4 pH 3 (remember that you always spell pH with a small 'p' and a capital 'H')
5 weak acid
6 toilet cleaner or oven cleaner
7 a substance that changes colour depending on whether an acid or an alkali is added to it
8 a pH 7; b pure water
9 a it won't change its colour; b pale green
10 your own answers

C2: Neutralisation

Get started: There are different ways of doing this but a good way is: car battery acid and oven cleaner (they are both strong but opposite. One is a strong acid and one is a strong alkali), orange juice and milk of magnesia (they are both weak), milk and seawater (they are both very weak). Have a look at the diagram of the pH scale on page 57 to help you see this.

1 when an acid cancels out an alkali
2 add an alkali
3 strong alkalis are dangerous
4 An acid is needed to neutralise wasp stings so they must be alkaline. They are the opposite to bee stings, so bee stings must be acidic.
5 Super Tummy since the least amount was needed to raise the pH above pH 6
6 antacid tablets of the different types, measuring cylinder, universal indicator, hydrochloric acid, spatula, beaker or cup, stirrer or spoon, safety glasses
7 How quickly can different antacids neutralise an acid? How many tablets of different antacids are needed to neutralise an acid? How much in grams of different antacids are needed to neutralise an acid?

C3: Solids, liquids and gases

Get started: Solids – sand, stone, wood; liquids – milk, water; gases – air, carbon dioxide, hydrogen.

1 a solids and liquids; b solids; c gases
2 a scientific idea that can be used to explain observations and data
3 saying what will happen in an investigation

4 Water, air, hydrogen, milk – there's a huge list of things that it could be; all gases and liquids can flow.
5 tiny particles that you can't see
6 There are lots of different answers to this: a good point might be that there would be no harmful acids or alkalis; a bad point might be that there would be no milk to drink; an interesting fact might be that life cannot exist without water.

C4: The particle theory

Get started: A grid of particles – always have a go at these Get started questions even if you're not sure if you're right – it will get your brain thinking in the right way!

1 a Magnesium is a solid, so:

b Helium is a gas, so:

c Mercury is a liquid, so:

2 a When particles of a liquid or a gas spread through another liquid or gas. b When a solid breaks up into particles that spread out through a liquid so you can't see solid pieces any longer.
3 It dissolves.
4 The air pressure outside the tin pushes on the walls of the tin. There is no air inside the tin to push back, so the tin crumples.
5 Your drawing should look a bit like this:

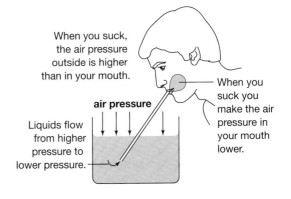

When you suck, the air pressure outside is higher than in your mouth.

air pressure

When you suck you make the air pressure in your mouth lower.

Liquids flow from higher pressure to lower pressure.

C5: Atoms and elements

Get started: They are all elements.

1 just like the diagram of the atoms in iron on page 64
2 a They both contain one type of atom. b The atoms they are made from are different.
3 any three non-elements (e.g. air, water, glass, paper, rock, salt, sand)
4 There are many correct answers – these are examples: Good point – we wouldn't need to separate elements from each other; bad point – there would be far fewer materials for us to use; interesting point – some elements exist for a fraction of a second when created by scientists.
5 atom, element
6 poor electrical and heat conductors, brittle, low melting points
7 on the right
8 your own answers

C6: Compounds and mixtures

Get started: It's not pure because it doesn't just contain one substance.

1 It contains more than one substance.
2 pure water (There are lots of others!)
3 Look at the diagram of particles in the air on page 66 and you'll see that there is also water and carbon dioxide in air – there are also tiny quantities of other gases such as xenon, neon, radon, krypton and helium.
4 Nitrogen – as you increase the temperature of liquid air up from −200 °C the first boiling point you get to is that of nitrogen.
5 ...a liquid is as hot as it can get.
6 a −196 °C; b −196 °C to −183 °C; c Allow it to heat up and if the hottest the liquid gets is 196 °C then it is pure. If the liquid gets hotter than this then it is not pure.
7 1064 °C (melting points and freezing points are always the same temperature)
8 No, because it is not pure and contains many different substances, all of which have their own melting points.

C7: Solutions

Get started: There are lots of possible answers. The best one is probably salt because all the others are insoluble in water and salt is soluble in water.

1 different substances jumbled up together
2 salt, sugar
3 The rest of the mass was the mass of the rock.
4 320 g
5 a A solute dissolved in a solvent. b You can't see through it. c You could name any suspension, e.g. muddy water, mayonnaise, hand cream, blood, paint.

6 insoluble, soluble, solution, solute, solvent
7 condensation

C8: More about dissolving

Get started: The only pure substance in the list is water, but remember that there are many different types of water (e.g. seawater, tap water, mineral water) and most of them are solutions. The only pure type of water is 'pure water' or 'distilled water'). The other liquids are all mixtures.

1 a substance made of only one material
2 a no; b The ink has separated into more than one colour. c ink D; d inks A and C
3 to check if there are things in it that should not be there
4 a a solution in which no more solute will dissolve; b Stir and add sugar until no more will dissolve and you can see undissolved sugar.
5 a sugar; b aspirin
6 a The solubility goes up. b 180 g/100 cm³ of water; c On the graph, if you put a ruler along the line showing the solubility of salt, you will see that at 100 °C the line crosses at about 39 g/100 cm³ of water or 40 g/100 cm³ of water; so the solubility of salt at 100 °C is about 39 or 40 g/100 cm³ of water.
7 The solubility of sugar is higher at hotter temperatures.
8 As the water cools the solubility of benzoic acid gets less and so not as much benzoic acid will dissolve in the water (some of the benzoic acid 'comes out of solution').

C9: Simple chemical reactions

Get started: In the ice cube you can freeze the water to get ice back. You can never get back raw egg from cooked egg.

1 No new materials are made in a physical change (most chemical reactions are irreversible, but not all). In a chemical reaction new substances are formed.
2 a reaction occurs/a gas is given off
3 water → steam – physical change, the rest are chemical reactions
4 hydrogen (the other product is magnesium chloride – you will learn about this another time)
5 carbon dioxide (the other products are water and calcium sulfate – you will learn about this another time)
6 a It explodes with a squeaky pop when ignited. b It turns limewater milky.
7 It goes out because the gas produced is carbon dioxide.

C10: Burning

Get started: Your labels should show that ash is made which cannot be turned back into wood, and that heat and light are given out which are both signs of a chemical reaction occurring.

1 A bright light and heat are given off and a new substance is formed.
2 Things burn better in 100% oxygen than in air which is only 20% oxygen.
3 calcium + oxygen → calcium oxide
4 something that contains a store of energy that can be changed into heat energy (usually when it is burned)
5 candle wax + oxygen → water + carbon dioxide
6 a The oxygen was used up. b The water took the place of the oxygen in the jar.
7 It cools the fire and takes away the heat (heat is one of the three things needed for combustion).
8 hydrogen + oxygen → water

C11: Making new materials

Get started: MgS (the metal always goes first).
1 Have a look in the glossary at the back of this book for the answers to this one!
2 Hydrogen is the obvious one but there are lots of others, including nitrogen and chlorine. (Remember that although water exists as molecules, it is *not* an element!)
3 a Carbon dioxide contains two oxygen atoms chemically joined to one carbon atom.
   b Hydrogen chloride contains one hydrogen atom chemically joined to one chlorine atom.
4 zinc oxide
5 water, carbon dioxide (there are plenty of others)
6 $CaCl_2$, HCl, KF
7 calcium, magnesium, carbon, oxygen
8 a hydrogen + chlorine → hydrogen chloride;
   b $H_2 + Cl_2 → 2HCl$ (the 2 in front of the chemical formula means '2 lots of');

c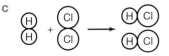

C12: Compounds

Get started: F_2, Ne, CO_2, He, CH_4 and Li; CO_2 and CH_4 are compounds.
1 Iron sulfide is not yellow and it sinks.
2 iron sulfide
3 molecules – carbon dioxide, hydrogen chloride, hydrogen oxide; blocks of atoms – iron sulfide, silver oxide, sodium chloride
4 a solution goes cloudy/changes colour; b heat is given out/bubbles appear, heat is given out or taken in
5 tiny particles of a solid
6 2

C13: Metals and metal compounds

Get started: Your own answer, which will probably include metals being strong, and some of the properties in the table on page 80.
1 carbon (in the form of graphite)
2 a drain covers, nails (there are many other things); b strong and cheap
3 It doesn't corrode very quickly and is very malleable.
4 It is lighter than copper.
5 a zinc chloride + hydrogen;
   b magnesium sulfate + hydrogen;
   c magnesium chloride + carbon dioxide + water; d calcium sulfate + carbon dioxide + water
6 Any three from: colour change, light given out, heat given out, heat taken in, bubbles of gas.

C14: More salts

Get started: There are lots of different kinds of salt.
1 a zinc chloride + water;
   b magnesium sulfate + water
2 a copper oxide + hydrochloric acid;
   b magnesium oxide + nitric acid;
   c zinc oxide + sulfuric acid;
   d calcium oxide + hydrochloric acid
3 making the pH of something neutral
4 pH 7
5 a pH 7;
   b hydrochloric acid + sodium hydroxide;
   c wear eye protection, do not touch liquids, wipe up spills immediately and immediately wash any chemicals you get on your skin with plenty of water
6 a sodium nitrate + hydrogen;
   b hydrochloric acid;
   c calcium carbonate, water;
   d hydrochloric acid, water;
   e potassium + hydrochloric acid;
   f zinc carbonate, carbon dioxide;
   g magnesium chloride + hydrogen

C15: Reactivity

Get started: Your own answer, but rust only happens to things that contain iron (e.g. pure iron, steel).
1 They react with water and/or gases in the air.
2 sodium (there are others, potassium for example)
3 calcium + water → calcium hydroxide + hydrogen
4 a potassium; b It has caught fire. c gold, copper, iron, zinc; d No bubbles are being produced. e hydrogen; f potassium hydroxide in water
5 a list of the metals in order of reactivity

C16: Using the reactivity series

Get started: Metal Y, metal X, metal Z
1 magnesium oxide
2 when a reactive metal takes the place of a less reactive metal in a compound
3 Copper is less reactive than iron.
4 **a** zinc sulfate + iron; **b** no reaction; **c** potassium nitrate + copper; **d** calcium sulfate + copper
5 It is too reactive (and reacts with water and oxygen around it).
6 It is too soft and reactive (it would fall apart the first time it rained).
7 Potassium, sodium, calcium and magnesium (zinc was discovered before the nineteenth century). The ones that were discovered in the nineteenth century are all very reactive so they weren't discovered before electricity was available to scientists.
8 **a** magnesium + hydrochloric acid → magnesium chloride + hydrogen; **b** There is an increase in temperature. **c** The reaction is finishing. **d** The reaction is over and no more heat is being produced but instead is being lost to the surroundings. **e** 22 °C; **f** The temperature would go up more because calcium is more reactive.
9 metal Y, zinc, metal X, copper (metal Y reacts with both solutions and so must be more reactive than both zinc and copper)

C17: Chemical reactions for energy

Get started: They are all fuels.
1 Trap some of the gas given off when burning methane and mix it with limewater – if it's carbon dioxide the limewater will go milky.
2 Your own ideas, but a good reason is that it produces no pollution (water is the only exhaust) and a bad reason is that it is a very dangerous fuel.
3 **a** CO; **b** C
4 So that they don't produce carbon monoxide which could harm people.
5 **a** C – zinc and gold; **b** electrical energy
6 aluminium + iron oxide → aluminium oxide + iron
7 **a i** zinc chloride + iron; **ii** no reaction; **iii** zinc nitrate + copper; **b** displacement reactions; **c** zinc + copper nitrate (because there is the greatest difference between the reactivities of the two metals, zinc and copper)

C18: Energy resources and new materials

Get started: They have all been made by chemical reactions.
1 Your own answer (e.g. to make a new medicine to treat a disease).
2 Mass is neither created nor destroyed.
3 hydrogen + oxygen → water, carbon + oxygen → carbon dioxide, hydrogen + chlorine → hydrogen chloride (note that it doesn't matter which way round you write the reactants so, oxygen + hydrogen → water is also correct)
4 **a** magnesium + oxygen → magnesium oxide; **b** It combines with oxygen which has a mass. **c** 17 g
5 water
6 **a** That materials contained phlogiston which escaped when they burned. **b** Phlogiston escaped so the wood had less mass. **c** burning magnesium (because that gains mass rather than losing it)

C19: Rocks and weathering

Get started: Your own answer.
1 minerals
2 rounded grains that don't fit together
3 a sharp-edged mineral grain
4 A, because water goes into the gaps between the grains, pushing out the air from the gaps.
5 **a** wearing away of rock; **b** biological, chemical, physical
6 Sandstone, because the acid that causes weathering can get inside a porous rock.
7 large rounded grains that don't fit together
8

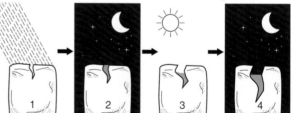

1: Rainwater gets into crack in rock. 2: Water freezes and expands, making crack bigger.
3: Ice melts and flows into deeper crack.
4: Water freezes again, making crack bigger still.

C20: Erosion and deposition

Get started: ...the rocks it can carry.
1 Rock fragments being carried away by water, wind or glacier (ice).
2 The water is flowing faster in the middle and can carry larger rocks, but any of these rocks that drift to the sides of the river will be deposited because the water is too slow there to carry them.

3   a layer B; b layer F; c conglomerate
4   Some seawater evaporated, leaving a layer of salt behind which was then covered in layers of sediment that turned to rock.

C21: Sedimentary and metamorphic rocks

Get started: Your own list.
1   compaction and cementation
2   a from prehistoric coral reef, from evaporating water, from a layer of shells; b Your own answer – finding the answer to this question here would be too easy!
3   a They all contain calcium carbonate and carbonates react with acids to produce carbon dioxide gas. b chalk; c oolite
4   limestone
5   a less porous; b The grains are squashed together more as the new rock forms.

C22: Igneous rocks

Get started: Forms solid rock
1   3 g/cm^3
2   Lava is magma on the Earth's surface.
3   a and b You should have added rocks like basalt (igneous), chalk (sedimentary), conglomerate (sedimentary), coquina (sedimentary), gabbro (igneous), gneiss (metamorphic), granite (igneous), limestone (sedimentary), marble (metamorphic), obsidian (igneous), oolite (sedimentary), quartzite (metamorphic), sandstone (sedimentary), tuff (igneous).
4   Igneous rocks are formed when molten rock solidifies. Sedimentary rocks are formed from layers of rock fragments and the remains of dead animals and plants which are squashed together. Metamorphic rocks are formed from igneous and sedimentary rocks when they are buried deep in the Earth and put under high pressures and temperatures.
5   W is sedimentary; has a texture of smooth, rounded grains; porous; could be sandstone; formed from layers of sediment. X is igneous; has a texture of large, interlocking crystals; not porous; could be granite; formed from magma cooling slowly. Y is metamorphic; has a texture of interlocking crystals in bands; not porous; could be gneiss; formed from igneous rock (granite) being changed by heat and pressure. Z is igneous; has a texture of small, interlocking crystals; not porous; could be basalt; formed from lava cooling quickly (remember that lava is magma that has reached the Earth's surface).

C23: Soils, rocks and acid rain

Get started: No, they are different – your evidence might include different colours, or some soils getting muddier than others when it rains, or some soils being more lumpy than others.
1   decaying parts of dead organisms
2   There are big gaps between the grains which water flows easily through.
3   a to grow crops that prefer more acidic soil; b lime
4   B – rainy with rain of pH 5.6
5   carbon dioxide, sulfur dioxide, nitrogen oxides
6   rain with a pH less than 5.6
7   Burn less fossil fuels is the answer but you might have written any of these too: fit sulfur precipitators to power station chimneys (to remove sulfur dioxide – see page 102); use petrol that has had sulfur removed; fit all cars with catalytic converters – see page 102. Some of these are dealt with on pages 102 and 103.

C24: Pollution and global warming

Get started: Cities produce more acidic gases, making rain in cities more acidic so it corrodes gravestones faster.
1   Limestone is made of a carbonate, which reacts with acids, but sandstone does not contain a carbonate.
2   water snail and Asellus
3   They reduce the amounts of acidic gases getting into the atmosphere.
4   problems caused by substances in the air
5   a traps the Earth's heat; b carbon dioxide, methane (there are others like nitrous oxide and CFCs)
6   a the heating up of Earth's atmosphere; b As the levels of carbon dioxide have risen, so has the Earth's temperature.
7   dirtiness of streets and buildings, thickness of smoke from factories
8   Examples include: don't waste electricity, travel on foot or on a bicycle rather than in a car, dispose of rubbish carefully, recycle what you can.

P1: Fossil fuels

Get started: Coal, petrol, natural gas, diesel
1 light, heat
2 sizes and types of all apparatus, amount of fuel, time of burning
3 a paraffin – 20 °C, ethanol – 19 °C, wood – 12 °C, firelighter – 44 °C; b firelighter; c It produced the biggest change in temperature.
4 A fuel formed from the dead remains of prehistoric animals and plants.
5 plants die; plants are buried; plant remains are squashed and heated and turn into coal
6 dead, tiny sea animals and plants
7 It takes millions of years to form and so can't be made again.
8 your own design

P2: Other energy resources

Get started: Renewable – geothermal, Sun, water, wind, wood; non-renewable – coal, oil.
1 a fuel made from a living thing
2 The Sun doesn't shine at night.
3 your own design, but it should involve a renewable energy resource
4 food
5 a 1265 kJ; b 506 000 apples
6

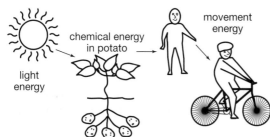

light energy → chemical energy in potato → movement energy

7 Use the apparatus shown on page 104 to burn the same mass of each breakfast cereal and measure the temperature rise of the water; the higher temperature rise would be given by the cereal with more energy.

P3: Hotter and colder

Get started: Freezing water is 0 °C; body temperature is 37 °C; boiling water is 100 °C; inside a fridge is usually about 4 °C; inside a freezer is usually about –20 °C.
1 It goes down.
2

heat energy

3 'Stone tiles *feel* colder than carpets.' or 'Stone tiles conduct heat away from my right foot more quickly than carpet so my right foot gets colder.'
4 The rod is metal but has only just started being heated and so one end is still cold/the rod is made from a material that is not a heat conductor.
5 It contains trapped air.
6 metal (or name of metal, e.g. iron)
7 Heat energy travelling by particles vibrating more and bumping into their neighbours.

P4: Heating and cooling

Get started: The ball gets bigger (expands) as it gets hotter.
1 The cooler particles have less energy so vibrate less and take up less room as they move around.
2 conduction, convection, radiation
3 There are convection currents in the water.
4 a Any example of house insulation, e.g. double glazing. b It contains trapped air (air is a poor conductor of heat by conduction and the air is trapped so that heat can't pass through it by convection).
5 into your skin
6 solid, liquid, gas
7 The heat energy is used to break the bonds holding the solid together rather than to increase the temperature.

P5: Light

Get started: Light and a hand. The shadow has a hand shape because the hand blocks out the light.
1 a The tube is bent. b straighten the tube; c Light travels in straight lines and so a straight tube will allow light to travel from the grass to her eye.
2 a It is transmitted through the glass. b It is absorbed by the blackboard.
3 does not produce its own light
4 Wood surface does not reflect light evenly.
5 34°
6 It can be absorbed or reflected.
7 It can be absorbed, reflected or transmitted.

P6: Colours of light

Get started: Your own masterpiece.
1 The bending of a ray of light as it goes from one material into a material with a different density.
2 outer space
3 The light ray bends away from the normal.
4 dispersion
5 magenta
6 The filter absorbs blue and red light and only allows green light to be transmitted.

7 Light	Shorts	T-shirt	Cap
a white	white	blue	red
b blue	blue	blue	black (red colours only reflect red light)
c red	red	black	red
d green	green	black	black
e magenta (remember that this contains both red and blue light)	magenta	blue	red

P7: Sounds

Get started: Your own answer.
1   how high or low a sound is
2   a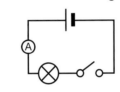

   b

3   a B; b C
4   The sound from wave Y is louder and lower in pitch than the sound from wave X (note that sounds have pitch and intensity whereas waves have frequency and amplitude).
5   The sound of the train moves faster through the solid rails than it does through the air.
6   The more ruler there is to vibrate, the lower the pitch of the note it makes.
7   It would travel more slowly.

P8: Hearing

Get started: Sound waves enter your ear and are changed into electrical signals that are sent to the brain.
1   eardrum, oval window
2   The person will become deaf.
3   a hertz; b decibels
4   Adults' ability to hear high pitches decreases with age – maybe because the bones in the middle ear can't vibrate as quickly as in a younger person.
5   to try to stop people damaging their hearing
6   your own answer

P9: Electrical circuits

Get started:

1   bulb/cell/resistor/switch
2   The switch is open so that there is a gap in the circuit.
3   a

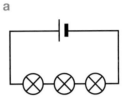

   b dimmer/less bright
4

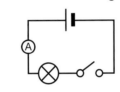

5   the 9 V cell
6   a plus end to minus end; b X – 2, Y – 3, Z – can't tell/lots

P10: More circuits

Get started: Same diagram as for the Get started on page 120!
1   Another bulb can be added **in parallel**.
    Although each bulb slows the flow of current, there are now two routes for the current to take and so the current in the main part of the circuit flows faster.

2   1 A
3   If you break a water pipe all the water flows out, but if you break a wire nothing flows out.
4   So that they all can be bright, or so that if one blows all the lights in the house don't go out.
5

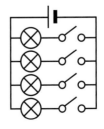

6 So that if something goes wrong and too much current flows through an appliance it doesn't catch fire.

7 a X – dimmer, Y – brighter, Z – normal (remember this is a parallel circuit – each loop has one bulb on it and each loop will allow the same current to go through it as if it were the only loop in the circuit); **b** L = 0.1 A (current does not get used up and is the same throughout a series circuit), M = 0.1 A, N = 0.9 A, O = 0.6 A, P = 0.3 A (the current divides to go down the different loops where the bulbs are and then joins up again)

P11: Energy transformations

Get started: Conduction, convection, radiation

1 Transferring energy is taking it from place to place; transforming is when the way in which energy is being transferred changes.

2 The way energy is being transferred changes from being transferred by an electrical current to being transferred by light waves and heating.

3

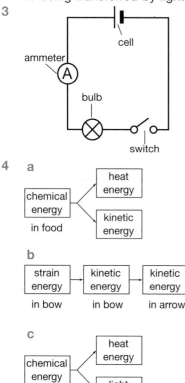

4 a

chemical energy in food → heat energy / kinetic energy

b

strain energy in bow → kinetic energy in bow → kinetic energy in arrow

c

chemical energy in candle wax → heat energy / light energy

Note: You may not have included the middle step in **b**.

5 a 3 V; **b** 1.5 V; **c** 3 V; **d** Current is not used up.

6 They can cause a large current to flow through you which can harm or kill you.

P12: Household electricity

Get started: The correct order is: electric clock, stereo, light bulb, television, toaster, tumble dryer. You don't need to remember or know this order, just know that some household appliances use much more electricity than others (especially those that heat things).

1

chemical energy in coal → heat energy in water/ steam → kinetic energy in turbine → electrical energy in generator

2 930 W

3 250 J

4 It is a greenhouse gas which traps heat energy in the Earth's atmosphere.

5 energy that is not useful

6

Device	Useful energy	Wasted energy
car	kinetic	heat, sound
hair dryer	heat, kinetic	sound
television	light, sound	heat
torch	light	heat

7 36%

8 a

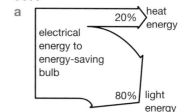

b The energy-saving light bulb would be less hot. **c** The energy-saving light bulb converts more energy into light rather than heat. **d** 80 J; **e** They use less electrical energy and so are cheaper to run.

9 12.5 J

P13: Different forces

Get started:

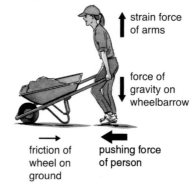

Don't worry if you didn't get all of these. Things to watch out for, though, are the fact that the arrows show not only the directions of forces but also their sizes – bigger arrow = bigger force.

1. **a** friction caused by something moving through air or water; **b** air resistance, water resistance
2. **a** a force that does not need to touch something to have an effect; **b** static electricity, magnetism, gravity
3. Your force arrow should point up and be labelled 'strain force' or 'force pulling up from forcemeter'.
4. forces that are equal in size and working in opposite directions
5. **a** To check that your measurements are right and you get reliable evidence. **b** If you double the weight you double the extension of the spring.

P14: Weight and friction

Get started: A standard apple has a mass of about 100 g and so it has a weight of 1 N (newtons). Six apples weigh about 6 N.
1. **a** 10 N; **b** 5 N; **c** 2 kg
2. reducing friction by using a lubricant
3. **a** about 16 N; **b** the block, the forcemeter, the person pulling the block, the weight of the block
4. **a** 12 metres; **b** miles per hour
5. Rainwater acts as a lubricant on the road and reduces the friction between the tyres and the road, so increasing the time it takes to stop.
6. There is not as much friction on ice as there is on a normal road surface.
7. Friction stops your feet slipping and sliding and so allows you to walk.
8. Your own answers, e.g. friction is useful on the feet of a ladder on a pavement; it is not useful when you go on a slide.

P15: Magnets and magnetism

Get started: Attract magnetic materials and, in some situations, repel other magnets.
1. **a** they will attract; **b** they will repel
2. Take a magnet and bring each pole in turn close to the iron. If the iron is a magnet, one end of the magnet will repel it.
3. Take a magnet and stroke the iron with it in the same direction lots of times.
4. nickel, iron, cobalt
5. the area around a magnet where a magnetic force can be felt
6. **a**

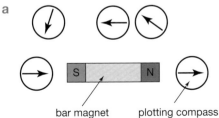

bar magnet   plotting compass

b They line up with the magnetic field going from north to south. **c** Move it well away from the magnet.

P16: Electromagnets

Get started: Something that is only a magnet when electricity flows through it.
1. increasing the number of coils, adding an iron core, increasing the current flowing through the coil/increasing the voltage
2. **a** the voltage/current and the type of core, the type of wire and the type and size of the paper clip
   b It could have been set to the wrong voltage; it might not have had 70 coils; some of the paper clips might have been different.
   c by repeating all the measurements
   d Use smaller things than paper clips to pick up (e.g. pins) and measure their mass (rather than number).
3. A magnetic field is produced.
4. **a** left-hand end; **b** Magnetic field lines always go from north to south pole.

P17: Gravity

Get started:

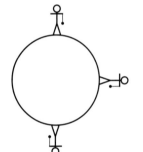

1. a force that exists between any two things that have mass, pulling them together
2. **a** 80 kg; **b** 800 N
3. 900 N
4. 62 kg
5. **a** 60 kg; **b** 60 kg (remember mass doesn't change)
6. **a** 1850 N; **b** 617 N; **c** The nearer two objects, the greater the force of gravity. (When the probe left Earth it lost weight as it moved further away from the Earth and then it gained weight again when it approached and landed on Mars. Note that it did not become 'weightless' between Earth and Mars – this is a misunderstanding that many people have – because it could still feel the gravity from Earth and from Mars but that gravity was very, very weak.)

P18: Speed

Get started: The correct order is: snail, tortoise, human, cheetah, car, jet aircraft.
1. **a** mph; **b** metres per year; **c** m/s; **d** km/h
2. **a** 10 m/s; **b** 20 km/h; **c** 20 mph; **d** 6 km/h
3. It speeds up.

4 a carry on at the same speed; b slow down;
   c speed up
5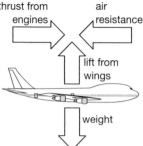
   thrust from engines
   air resistance
   lift from wings
   weight

6 a change in speed (note that a positive
   acceleration is speeding up and a negative
   acceleration is slowing down – often called a
   deceleration)

P19: Speeding up and slowing down

Get started: Your own design but it should look smooth and streamlined.

1 air resistance, water resistance
2 a Making an object smooth so that air or
   water can flow easily around it. b Streamlining
   reduces air resistance and so less force from
   the engine is needed to make a vehicle go at a
   certain speed.
3 a the one that went at 70 mph; b The faster a
   vehicle goes, the more air resistance, which is
   caused by particles hitting the vehicle, and the
   more particles that hit it the hotter it gets.
4 C and E
5 The air resistance is greater than his weight.
6 Air resistance and weight are balanced forces.
7 It doesn't change.
8 a 50 m/s; b at 15 seconds

P20: Pressure

Get started: The nail heads are sharp and so have a greater pressure that causes them to dig into your back.

1 the amount of force on a certain area
2 a 5 N/cm²; b 5 N/m² or 5 Pa
3 to stop them sinking into the sand
4 a $P = \dfrac{F}{A}$ (force *divided by* area)

   $= \dfrac{250}{2} = 125$ N/cm²;

   b 125 N/cm² (the pressure doesn't change
   through the liquid); c F = P × A (look at the
   triangle on page 142 and cover up the F, which
   tells you that to work out F you have to multiply
   P by A) = 125 × 6 = 750 N; d the left-hand one
   (the force is increased in a hydraulic system at
   the expense of the distance moved)

5 The air will squash and so not pass on the
   pressure through the liquid.
6 The pressure is greatest at the bottom.
7 The pressure increases and squashes it.
8 There is less pressure pushing on the walls of
   the balloon from the air at the top of Everest
   (the air pressure gets less the higher you go), so
   the air in the balloon can expand.
9 The wall needs to hold up against a much
   greater pressure at the bottom.

P21: Moments

Get started: It is easier to push the door open next to the handle. Handles are placed on doors so that you have to apply as little force as possible to open them.

1 the turning motion that a force can cause
2 a moment = force × distance
   = 70 × 0.2 = 14 N m;
   b force = moment/distance (moment *divided by*
   distance) = = 1400 N (again remember to work
   in metres). You could think up a triangle (like
   the ones for pressure and density) to remember
   how to work out moments.
3 a The pivot is where the two blades join.
   b More force is generated closer to the pivot.
4 (work in newtons and metres because the units
   for a moment are newton metres)
   a Chantelle: moment = force × distance
   = 500 × 1.5 = 750 N m (don't forget the units).
   Anna: moment = force × distance
   = 500 × 1.5 = 750 N m. The moments are the
   same and so the see-saw will balance.
   b Dave: moment = 450 × 2 = 900 N m.
   Michael: moment = 300 × 3 = 900 N m.
   The moments are the same and so the see-saw
   will balance.
   c Taylor: moment = 600 × 1.5 = 900 N m.
   Courtney: moment = 400 × 2 = 800 N m. The
   moments are not the same and the see-saw will
   not balance.

P22: Sun, Moon and Earth

Get started: Your diagram should show a light ray or light rays from the Sun being reflected by the Moon towards the Earth. Part of the diagram at the top of page 147 shows this. The Moon shines because it reflects sunlight.

1 The Earth's axis is tilted which gives us
   seasons. In winter the Northern hemisphere
   points away from the Sun and so spends more
   time in darkness. Days are shorter in winter and
   so it is colder. When it's winter in the UK it's
   summer in the Southern hemisphere.
2 a the path something takes around something
   else; b the imaginary line running through the
   Earth from pole to pole; c half of the Earth

3 a All of the side of the Moon facing us is sunlit and so it's very bright. b Most of the Moon's surface facing us is in darkness and so it's not very bright.

c

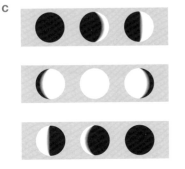

4 because it goes dark

5

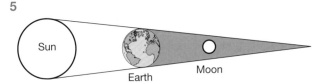

P23: The Solar System

Get started: Your own list – have a look at all the words in bold on pages 146 to 149.

1 Mars
2 165 Earth years
3 a They get colder. b They are further from the heat of the Sun.
4 the galaxy that our Sun is in
5 It is the only body in the Solar System that has water, oxygen and a suitable temperature.
6 The Earth is rotating.
7 your own questions!

P24: Space

Get started: Your sketch should show the Sun with eight planets circling around it in this order: Mercury, Venus, Earth, Mars, Jupiter, Saturn, Uranus, Neptune. You might have included some of the dwarf planets like Pluto and Ceres.

1 Rockets go through the sky; satellites show us that the Earth is round like a ball.
2 It should explain all the evidence and be able to make accurate predictions.
3 Kepler said that the planets had elliptical (oval-shaped) orbits.
4 the Moon
5 an object that orbits a planet
6 a geostationary; b polar; c geostationary

Glossary

abdomen Rear section of an insect body.

abrasion When rock fragments bash into each other and become smoother as they are moved from place to place.

absorb Take in.

acceleration A change in speed (e.g. speeding up).

accuracy Correctness.

acid Liquid that has a pH of less than 7.

acid rain Rain with a pH of less than 5.6.

adaptation A feature that helps an organism to survive in a certain habitat.

addictive An addictive substance causes a feeling that the person must have it.

adolescence When physical and emotional changes occur in teenagers.

aerobic respiration Chemical reaction that releases energy from glucose using oxygen.

afterbirth The placenta when pushed out after a birth.

air resistance Friction caused by things moving through air.

alcoholic Someone who depends on alcohol.

alkali A soluble base. Often found as a liquid with a pH of greater than 7.

alveolus Tiny sac found in lungs, where gas exchange occurs. Plural = alveoli.

ammeter Used to measure an electrical current.

amnion Bag that contains amniotic fluid.

amniotic fluid Liquid protecting a growing fetus.

amp (A) Unit for electrical current.

amphibian Vertebrate with a body covered in moist skin.

amplitude The amplitude of a wave is how tall it is.

angle of incidence Angle at which a light ray hits a mirror.

angle of reflection Angle at which a light ray bounces off a mirror.

antacid Weakly alkaline medicine to treat heartburn.

antagonistic pair Pair of muscles that pull a bone in opposite directions.

antennae Long parts on an insect used to sense things.

antibiotic Medicine that kills bacteria.

antibody Substance made by white blood cells that can destroy harmful bacteria and viruses.

anus Ring of muscle holding faeces inside the body until they need to be eliminated.

arachnid Arthropod with eight legs and two body parts.

artery Blood vessel that carries blood away from the heart.

arthropod Invertebrate with jointed legs, a hard outer skeleton and a body divided into sections.

artificial satellite Something made by humans that is in orbit around a planet (e.g. a TV satellite orbiting the Earth).

asteroid belt Region where there are lots of asteroids.

asteroid Lump of rock in space.

atom The smallest part of a substance. We think of atoms as tiny, tiny spheres.

attract Pull together.

auditory nerve Nerve that carries electrical signals from the cochlea to the brain.

average speed *See* mean speed.

axis Imaginary line through Earth from pole to pole.

bacteria Microbes made of only one cell. Bigger than viruses, smaller than yeasts.

balanced diet Eating all the different nutrients in the right amounts.

balanced forces When two forces on something are equal in size and opposite in direction.

bar chart Data shown as bars that vary in height.

basalt Igneous rock formed when lava cools quickly.

base Substance that reacts with acids in a neutralisation reaction.

battery Two or more electrical cells connected together.

bile Liquid that helps to digest fats.

bioaccumulation The gradual build-up of a substance in the bodies of animals as you move along a food chain.

biological weathering Rocks being worn away by living things.

biomass New material that an organism makes as it grows.

biomass fuel Fuel made from a living thing.

bird Vertebrate with a body covered in feathers.

bladder Organ that stores urine.

blood pressure The pressure of blood in blood vessels. High blood pressure damages the blood vessels which can then cause heart disease, heart attacks, kidney failure, etc.

blood vessel Tube that carries blood in the body.

boiling point Temperature at which a liquid will be as hot as it can get.

bond Force that holds particles together.

braking distance The distance a car travels from when a driver presses the brake pedal until the car actually stops.

breathing Muscles moving to make your lungs bigger and smaller.

breathing system All the organs needed for breathing (e.g. lungs, diaphragm, trachea (windpipe)). Also called the respiratory system.

breed Group of animals of the same species that share similar characteristics.

bulb Turns electrical energy into light energy.

Bunsen burner Used to heat things in a lab.

caffeine Stimulant drug found in cola, tea and coffee.

calcium Mineral needed for healthy teeth and bones.

capillary Smallest sort of blood vessel that allows the fluid containing oxygen and glucose to leak out of the blood to get to the tissues.

carbohydrate Nutrient in food used for energy.

carbon dioxide Greenhouse gas produced by respiration and used in photosynthesis.

carbon monoxide Poisonous gas found in cigarette

smoke and formed in gas appliances that do not have a good source of air.

carbonate A type of chemical that reacts with acids to give off carbon dioxide gas.

carbonate-rich Containing a lot of compounds called carbonates.

carnivore Organism that only eats other animals.

carpel The female sexual organ in flowering plants.

catalytic converter Component fitted to car exhausts that changes nitrogen oxides into nitrogen.

cell Basic building-block of all organisms.

cell division Process in which a cell splits to make two identical copies.

cell sap Liquid inside a plant cell vacuole.

cell surface membrane Thin covering of a cell.

cell wall Box that protects and supports plant cells.

cellulose Substance used to make plant cell walls.

cementation Process in which minerals in sediment 'glue' grains of sediment together.

centipede Arthropod with more than 14 jointed legs, one pair on each of many body sections.

cervix Ring of muscle that holds a fetus in the uterus.

chamber Large space inside the heart that fills with blood.

characteristics Features of an organism.

chemical energy Energy stored in materials (e.g. food).

chemical formula Shorthand way of writing down the name of a compound using symbols.

chemical reaction Change that makes new materials.

chemical symbol One or two letter shorthand for a chemical's name.

chemical weathering Chemicals wearing away rocks.

chlorophyll Green substance used for photosynthesis in chloroplasts.

chloroplast Green disc inside plant cells.

chromatogram The result of chromatography.

chromatography A way of separating different solutes.

cilia Hairs on some cells that sweep things along.

ciliated epithelial cells Cells with hairs (cilia) on them that wave to sweep things along.

circulatory system Set of organs involved in moving blood around the body.

classification Grouping organisms based on features.

clay soil Soil containing tiny particles. Holds water well.

coal Fossil fuel formed from dead plants.

cochlea Coiled tube used to detect sound waves inside your ear.

colony Large group of organisms (e.g. bacteria) growing together.

combustion Scientific word for burning.

comet Lump of rock and ice that speeds through space.

community All the organisms living in a habitat.

compaction Process in which a layer of sediment is squashed and water is squeezed out from between the grains.

competition When organisms have to struggle with one another for their share of a resource (e.g. light, food, mineral salts).

complete circuit An electrical circuit with no gaps.

component Part in an electrical circuit (e.g. a bulb).

compound Substance containing more than one kind of atom chemically joined together.

compress Squash.

condensation Turning from a gas into a liquid.

condensing Turning a gas into a liquid.

conduction When heat energy travels by particles vibrating more and bumping into their neighbours.

conglomerate Sedimentary rock formed from pebbles.

conifers Group of plants with needle-shaped leaves that reproduce using seeds found in cones.

constellation Imaginary grouping of stars.

consumer Organism that eats other organisms.

contact force Force that only exists when things touch.

contracts Gets smaller.

control Part of an investigation where the factor being tested is left out.

convection When heat energy travels by liquids and gases becoming more or less dense than their surroundings.

convection current Movement of a gas or a liquid caused by some areas of the gas or liquid being less dense than other areas.

coral reef Structure made from the skeletons of animals called corals.

correlation Link between two things; so that if one thing is changed the other changes.

corrode When a chemical reaction destroys part of something.

corrosive Will attack your body, especially your skin.

coverslip Thin piece of glass placed on a specimen.

crop Plant grown to produce something useful (e.g. food, cotton).

cross-breeding When two organisms from different breeds or varieties are bred together.

crustacean Type of arthropod with a chalky shell and five to seven pairs of legs. A lobster is an example.

crystal Sharp-edged grain of a mineral.

current Flow of electricity.

cuticle Waxy layer on leaves to stop them drying out.

cytoplasm Where new substances are made in a cell.

daily change Change in a habitat happening every day.

data Information.

datalogger Piece of equipment that can record the numbers from sensors attached to it.

day When light from the Sun reaches part of the Earth. 'A day' is the time for the Earth to turn once on its axis.

decibel (dB) Unit for measuring the intensity of a sound.

deficiency disease Disease caused by a lack of a nutrient.

degrees Celsius (°C) Unit for measuring temperature.

density The mass of a unit volume of something (e.g. the mass of 1 cm³, which would commonly have units g/cm³).

deposition Dropping of sediment by a river, stream, glacier or wind.

depressant A drug that decreases the activity of nerves.

diaphragm Sheet of muscle used in breathing.

diet What you eat.

diffusion The natural spreading of particles of a liquid or a gas through another liquid or gas.

digest Break down.

digestive system Organs involved in breaking down and absorbing food.

dilution Adding water to something.

dispersion Splitting of light into the colours of the spectrum.

displacement reaction Reaction in which a reactive metal takes the place of a less reactive metal in a compound.

dissolving The breaking up of a solid in a liquid.

distance–time graph Graph showing how distance changes over time.

distillation Evaporation followed by condensation. Used to separate a solvent from a solution.

distribution Where an organism can be found in different parts of a habitat.

drag Friction caused by things moving in gases (e.g. air resistance) and liquids (e.g. water resistance).

drug Chemical that alters the way part of the body works.

ear canal Channel leading from outside into your ear.

eardrum Sheet of very thin 'skin' at the end of the ear canal.

Earth The third planet from the Sun in the Solar System.

echinoderm Invertebrate with a body in five parts.

ecologist A scientist who investigates habitats.

efficiency The percentage of energy that is changed into useful energy by something.

egg cell Female sex cell.

electric shock Pain caused by electricity flowing in you.

electrical conductor Material that allows electricity through it easily.

electrical energy Energy carried by an electrical current.

electromagnet Coil of wire with an electrical current flowing through it.

element Substance containing only one kind of atom.

eliminate Get rid of.

embryo Clump of cells that grow into a new organism.

energy flow diagram Flow chart showing energy changes.

energy resource Thing used to produce useful energy.

engulf Surround and take in.

environment Conditions in a habitat (e.g. temperature).

environmental variation A characteristic that has been caused by something in the surroundings.

enzyme Substance that speeds up chemical reactions in the body.

equator Imaginary line around the middle of the Earth.

erosion When fragments of weathered rocks are moved.

estimate Judge the numbers of something without doing accurate counting.

evaporation Turning from a liquid into a gas.

exhalation Using muscles to breathe out.

expand Get bigger.

eyepiece lens The microscope lens you look through.

factor Thing that can alter the results you get in an investigation. You normally change one factor and keep all the others the same.

faeces Undigested food.

fair test An investigation when you only change one thing.

fat Nutrient in food used for energy storage and heat insulation.

feeding relationship Way in which one organism depends on another for food.

female reproductive system All the organs that are used for reproduction in females.

fermentation Type of respiration carried out by yeast which makes alcohol.

ferns Group of plants with roots and xylem that reproduce using spores.

fertilisation When a male and a female sex cell join together (or fuse).

fertilised egg cell Cell formed during fertilisation.

fetus An embryo that has developed arms and legs.

fibre Indigestible food substance that keeps your guts healthy.

filter 'A filter' is something used to separate insoluble substances from a liquid. 'To filter' is to use a filter.

fish Vertebrate with a body covered in wet scales.

flammable Will easily catch fire.

flower Plant organ that makes seeds.

flowering plants Group of plants with broad, flat leaves and flowers. They reproduce using seeds found in fruits.

focusing wheel Wheel used to focus a microscope.

food chain A diagram showing what eats what in a habitat.

food web A diagram made up of many joined food chains to show what eats what in a habitat.

fossil Remains of a dead organism, often millions of years old.

fossil fuel Fuel formed over millions of years from dead organisms.

fractional distillation Distilling a mixture of liquids to separate them based on their boiling points.

freeze–thaw action When water freezes and melts over and over making cracks in rocks bigger.

freezing Turning a liquid into a solid.

freezing point Temperature at which a substance changes from a liquid into a solid. The same as its melting point.

frequency The frequency of a wave is how many complete waves pass a point each second.

friction A contact force that pulls back on things sliding past each other.

fruit Something made by flowering plants that contains or carries a seed.

fuel Something that can be made to give out heat energy (usually by burning it).

fulcrum Another name for 'pivot'.

full moon When we can see all the lit side of the Moon.

function Another word for a 'job'.

fungi Mushrooms are fungi but so are some tiny single-celled organisms which are microbes (e.g. yeasts).

fuse (biology) To join together.

fuse (physics) Contains a wire that melts if too much current flows.

gabbro Igneous rock formed when lava cools slowly underground.

galaxy Group of millions of stars in space.

gall bladder Pocket that releases bile.

galvanise Coating iron with zinc so that the iron does not rust.

gas exchange Transferring oxygen and carbon dioxide into and out of the blood.

gas State of matter. Gases flow, take up the shapes and volumes of their containers and can be squashed.

gene Made of a substance called DNA and where genetic information is stored.

generator A magnet inside a coil of wire. An electrical current is produced in the wire when the magnet is turned.

genetic information Information that is stored in the nuclei of cells and that controls what characteristics an organism will have.

geostationary orbit Orbit in which a satellite remains over a fixed place on the Earth.

geothermal power Electricity produced when water is turned to steam underground and used to turn a turbine.

gestation The time between fertilisation and birth.

glands Pockets in the body that produce liquids.

global warming Heating up of the Earth's atmosphere.

glucose Sugar made by photosynthesis and used up in respiration.

gneiss Metamorphic rock formed from granite.

grain Particle found in rocks and made of a mineral.

gram (g) Unit of mass.

granite Igneous rock normally containing black, white and pink-coloured minerals. Formed when lava cools slowly underground.

gravitational potential energy Energy stored in something that can fall.

gravity Force that exists between any two things that have mass, pulling them together (e.g. the Earth and you).

greenhouse gas Gas in the atmosphere that traps heat.

gut Collection of organs that your food travels through.

habitat Area where organisms live (e.g. sea, woodland).

harmful Will damage a part of your body.

hazard symbol Drawing that warns about dangerous chemicals.

head Front or top section of an animal's body.

heart Organ that pumps blood.

heart disease Disease when some cells in the heart don't get enough food or oxygen from the blood and start to die off.

heat conductor Same as thermal conductor.

heat energy The energy that makes things hot and causes the particles in substances to vibrate more.

heat insulator Same as thermal insulator.

hemisphere Half the Earth.

herbicide Chemical that kills plants. Also called a weedkiller.

herbivore Organism that only eats plants.

hertz (Hz) Unit for measuring the frequency of a sound wave.

hibernation Going to sleep for the winter.

hormone Chemical made in your body that causes changes.

humus Decaying dead parts of organisms.

hydraulic Filled with liquid.

hydrocarbon Chemical made of only hydrogen and carbon.

hydroelectric power Electricity produced when water flows out of a reservoir and turns turbines.

hydrogencarbonate indicator Indicator that turns different colours depending on how much carbon dioxide there is.

hypothesis Scientific idea about why or how something happens.

igneous rock Rock formed when magma (or lava) cools.

immune If you can't get a disease you are 'immune' to it.

immunisation Making people immune to diseases.

implantation When an embryo sticks in the uterus lining.

impure Material that contains a chemical mixed with other things.

infected When a person has a disease caused by a microbe.

infection When a microbe causes a disease in you.

infectious disease Disease that can be spread between people.

inhalation Using muscles to breathe in.

inherited Characteristics passed from parents to offspring are said to be 'inherited'.

inherited variation Characteristic inherited from a parent.

insect Arthropod with six legs and three body parts.

insoluble Something that does not dissolve.

intensity Loudness of a sound.

interlocking crystals Sharp-edged pieces of minerals that fit together without leaving gaps.

interlocking texture Rock texture in which crystals fit together without leaving gaps between them.

internal pressure The pressure inside a liquid or a gas.

The more liquid or gas there is above you, the more pressure there is.

invertebrates Animals that don't have backbones.

iodine solution Brown liquid that turns blue/black if added to starch.

iron Mineral needed for healthy blood.

irreversible change Change that cannot be reversed.

irritant Will make a part of your body hurt.

joint Part of the body where bones are moved by muscles.

joule (J) Unit for measuring energy (J).

Jupiter Fifth planet from the Sun in the Solar System.

kilojoule (kJ) One thousand joules. 1000 J = 1 kJ.

kinetic energy Energy that a moving thing has. Also called 'movement energy'.

kingdoms Largest groups living things are sorted into.

large intestine Organ that absorbs water from undigested food.

lava Magma that reaches the surface of the Earth.

law of conservation of energy Energy cannot be created or destroyed, only transformed from one type into another.

law of conservation of mass Mass is neither created nor destroyed.

leaf Plant organ that makes food.

leap year A year on Earth in which an extra day is added.

lever Simple machine that uses a pivot to change the direction and size of a force.

ligament Tissue that links bones together.

light energy Energy given out by luminous sources.

light ray Straight line showing direction in which light travels.

lime Crushed calcium carbonate added to soil to make it less acidic.

limestone Sedimentary rock often formed from the shells and skeletons of sea creatures.

limewater Clear, colourless liquid that goes 'milky' when carbon dioxide is added.

line graph Data shown as a line going from one point to the next point.

line of best fit Straight line that goes the best way through all the points on a scatter graph.

liquid Liquids flow, take up the shapes of their containers, keep their volumes, cannot be squashed.

litmus Indicator. Turns red in acids and blue in alkalis.

loam Mixture of clay soil and sandy soil.

lubricant Something that reduces friction.

luminous source Something that produces its own light.

lunar eclipse When the Earth blocks light from the Sun reaching the Moon.

lunar month Time for the Moon to orbit the Earth once.

lung Organ than takes oxygen out of the air and puts carbon dioxide into it.

lysozyme Enzyme in tears that destroys microbes.

machine A device that can change the direction and/or the size of a force.

magma Liquid rock.

magnet Something that can create a magnetic force around it.

magnetic field Area around a magnet where a magnetic force is felt.

magnetic materials Materials that can be attracted to magnets.

magnetism The force between two magnets or a magnet and a magnetic material.

magnify To make something appear bigger.

mains electricity Electricity supplied to homes and factories along wires.

male reproductive system All the organs that are used for reproduction in males.

mammal Vertebrate with a body covered in hair.

marble Metamorphic rock formed from limestone.

Mars Fourth planet from the Sun in the Solar System.

mass The amount of matter in something.

mean A type of average in which all of a set of repeated readings are added together and then divided by the number of readings.

mean speed Average speed over a period of time, found by dividing the total distance travelled by the total time taken.

medicine Drug used to treat a disease or condition (either to help cure it or to relieve the symptoms).

melting Turning a solid into a liquid.

melting point Temperature at which a substance changes from a solid into a liquid. The same as its freezing point.

menstrual cycle Cycle in women that causes egg cells to be released and the uterus lining to be replaced.

menstruation The passing of the lining of the uterus out through the vagina in women.

Mercury Planet closest to the Sun in our Solar System.

metal Element that conducts heat and electricity and can be stretched and dented.

metal oxides Compound of a metal with oxygen.

metamorphic rock Rock that is changed by being squashed and/or heated to extremely high temperatures under the Earth.

methane The gas found in natural gas.

micro-organism Another name for a microbe.

microbe Tiny living thing that you need a microscope to see.

microscope A device that magnifies small things.

migration Going to another place for a season.

Milky Way The galaxy that our Sun is in.

milligram (mg) A thousandth of a gram = 0.001 g.

millipede Arthropod with more than 14 jointed legs, two pairs on each of many body sections.

mineral (biology) Nutrient in food that you need tiny amounts of to stay healthy, e.g. calcium is used to make strong bones and teeth.

mineral (chemistry) Type of chemical that rocks are made of.

mineral salts Salts that don't contain carbon, such as sodium nitrate and calcium phosphate. Many mineral salts are important, in small quantities for plant growth and so are found in fertilisers.

mirror Flat shiny surface that reflects light evenly.

mitochondria Tiny structures in the cytoplasm of cells in which respiration occurs. Singular = mitochondrion.

mixture Two or more different kinds of elements or compounds that are jumbled up together – not chemically joined to each other.

model Familiar thing that can be used to think about what happens in an unfamiliar thing.

molecule One atom linked to one or more other atoms.

mollusc Invertebrate with a single fleshy muscle to move.

moment Turning effect of a force, calculated by multiplying the force by the perpendicular distance of the force from the pivot.

moon A rocky sphere that orbits a planet. The Moon orbits the Earth.

mosses Group of plants with no roots or xylem that reproduce using spores.

mucus Sticky liquid made in the body.

mucus plug Forms at the entrance to the cervix during pregnancy, to keep infections away from the developing fetus.

mudstone Sedimentary rock formed from mud grains.

muscle tissue Lots of muscle cells grouped together.

natural defences Your body's ways of keeping out microbes and destroying them to keep you healthy.

natural gas A fossil fuel formed when oil forms.

natural satellite Rocky object orbiting a planet; the Moon is Earth's natural satellite

Neptune The furthest planet from the Sun.

nerve cell Another name for a neurone.

neurone Cell that carries information around the body using electrical impulses.

neutral Liquid that has a pH of 7.

neutralisation When an acid and an alkali cancel out.

new moon When we cannot see the lit side of the Moon.

newton (N) Unit for force.

newton metre (N m) The unit for the turning effect (moment) of a force.

nicotine Addictive drug in tobacco (cigarettes) that causes high blood pressure and heart disease.

night When sunlight is not reaching a part of the Earth.

nitrates Salts that are very important for plant growth. They can be made artificially using nitric acid. Nitrate salts contain a nitrate group of atoms (nitrogen and oxygen).

nitrogen oxides Compounds of nitrogen and oxygen. These are acidic gases that can dissolve in rainwater and form acid rain.

nocturnal Active at night.

non-contact force Force that works even if two things aren't touching.

non-element Substance that contains more than one kind of atom.

non-luminous Does not produce its own light.

non-luminous source Something that does not produce its own light.

non-metal Element that doesn't conduct electricity (except graphite) and is brittle so can't be stretched or dented.

non-renewable Energy resource that cannot be remade.

normal A line drawn at right angles to the point where a light ray meets a mirror. It is used to help measure the angles.

north pole Pole of a magnet that points North if the magnet is allowed to turn freely.

North pole The top of the northern hemisphere.

Northern hemisphere Half the Earth above the equator.

nuclear energy Energy inside atoms, especially in radioactive atoms.

nucleus The control centre of a cell.

nutrients Raw materials found in food that give you energy and keep you healthy.

nutrition information Information on food packets about what the food contains.

obesity Being very overweight.

objective lens Microscope lens closest to the specimen.

observation Looking carefully at something.

obsidian Igneous rock formed when lava solidifies very, very quickly.

offspring Young organisms produced by parents.

oil Fossil fuel formed from small dead sea organisms.

opaque Opaque substances don't let light through them.

orbit The path of something around another thing.

organ Different tissues grouped together.

organ system Set of organs working together.

organism Living thing.

oscilloscope Device used to display sound waves as 'up and down waves'.

oval window Sheet of very thin 'skin' at the entrance to the cochlea in your ear.

ovary Part of a female that produces egg cells.

oviduct Tube that carries egg cells towards the uterus.

ovulation When an ovary releases an egg cell.

ovule Bag that contains an egg cell in a flower.

oxide Compound made of atoms of oxygen and another element.

palisade cells Cells near the surface of a leaf, packed with chloroplasts, in which photosynthesis takes place.

pancreas Organ that makes enzymes to digest food.

parallel Circuit where each electrical component is connected on its own loop of wire.

particle theory Idea that all matter is made of tiny, moving particles.

pascal (Pa) The unit for pressure. $1 \text{ Pa} = 1 \text{ N/m}^2$.

peat Fossil fuel that can turn into coal.

penis Male organ used to put semen into a female.

Periodic Table Way of arranging the elements.

pest Organism that damages crops.

pesticide Chemical used to kill organisms that damage crops.

pH scale Scale of strengths of acids and alkalis.

phases of the Moon Series of shapes caused by us seeing different amounts of the sunlit side of the Moon.

phlogiston theory Old theory about burning, which said that substances that burn contained phlogiston. According to the theory, when they burned they lost phlogiston and so lost mass.

phosphates Compounds that are important for plant growth. Phosphates include a phosphate group of atoms (phosphorus and oxygen).

photosynthesis Process that plants use to make food.

physical change Change in which no new materials are made.

physical environmental factor Non-living feature of a habitat (e.g. temperature, amount of rain).

physical weathering When forces wear away rocks.

pitch How high or low a musical note or sound is.

pivot Point about which something can turn, such as the hinge on a door.

placenta Disc that takes oxygen and food from a mother's blood to give to a developing fetus. It passes the fetus's waste back to the mother's blood.

plasma Liquid part of the blood.

Pluto A dwarf planet in the Solar System.

pneumatic Filled with air.

polar orbit Orbit in which a satellite travels over both poles.

pole One end of a magnet where its magnetic force is strongest.

pole The top or bottom of the Earth.

pollen grain Male sex cell in plants.

pollen tube Tube that grows from a pollen grain.

pollination When a pollen grain lands on a stigma.

pollution When substances in an environment cause problems.

population The total number of an organism living in a habitat.

porous Lets water through.

potassium Reactive element whose mineral salt compounds are needed by plants.

potential energy Energy that is stored.

power rating Number of joules of energy something uses each second. Measured in watts (W). 1 W = 1 J/s.

precipitate Fine particles of a solid formed in a liquid during a chemical reaction.

predator Animal that eats other animals.

prediction What you think will happen in an investigation.

premature Early.

pressure Amount of force on a certain area.

prey Animal that is eaten by other animals.

primary colours of light Red, blue and green light can be combined in different amounts to give all the other colours of light.

producer Organism that makes its own food (e.g. a plant).

products The materials you end up with after a chemical reaction.

property How a material behaves.

protein Nutrient in food used for growth and repair.

puberty Time when physical changes occur in teenagers.

pure When a substance is made of only one material.

pyramid of numbers Way of showing the numbers of organisms in a food chain as bars stacked on top of each other.

quadrat Square frame used for sampling a habitat.

quartzite Metamorphic rock formed from sandstone.

radiation When heat travels without needing particles.

raw material Something that's used to make other things out of.

reactants The materials you start with before a chemical reaction.

reaction time The time taken to respond to something happening.

reactive A substance that reacts easily is reactive.

reactivity series A list of metals in order of how reactive they are.

recreational drug Drug taken for pleasure.

reflect Bounce off.

reflection When light bounces off a surface.

refraction The bending of a ray of light as it goes from one material into a material with a different density.

relax When something stops contracting it relaxes.

reliable Results or data that you can be sure of. Using bigger sample sizes and repeating readings are two ways to get more reliable data.

reliability How sure you are that the results of an investigation were obtained correctly.

renewable An energy resource that will not run out.

repel Push apart.

reproduction When new organisms are created.

reptile Vertebrate with a body covered in dry scales.

resistance A property that slows down electric current.

respiration Chemical reaction that releases energy from a carbohydrate called glucose.

respiratory system Another name for the breathing system. All the organs needed for breathing (e.g. lungs, diaphragm, windpipe).

reversible change Change which can be reversed so that you can get back the materials that you started with.

rock cycle All the processes that make and change the three different types of rocks.

rock salt Mixture of rock and salt mined from the ground.

root Plant organ that takes in water and anchors a plant.

root hair cell Plant cell that is adapted to absorb water quickly from the ground by having a finger-like extension.

root hair tissue Lots of root hair cells grouped together.

saliva Liquid made in mouth to help digest starch and make food easier to swallow.

salivary glands Pockets in the mouth that make saliva.

salt Compound that consists of a metal attached to a chloride, sulfate or nitrate 'group'.

sample size The number of measurements of the same type taken in an investigation.

sampling Looking at a small part of a big area to work out what the whole of the area is like.

sandstone Yellow-coloured sedimentary rock formed from grains of sand.

sandy soil Soil containing large particles. Water drains through it.

satellite Something that is in orbit around a planet.

saturated solution Solution that can dissolve no more solute.

Saturn Sixth planet from the Sun in the Solar System.

scab Dried blood sealing a cut.

scatter graph Data shown as points on a graph. A line of best fit is often drawn through these points. A scatter graph is used to try to find a correlation between two variables.

scrotal sac Bag of skin that holds the testes.

season Time of year when the weather behaves in a certain way.

seasonal change Habitat change that occurs each year.

sediment Bits of rock carried by a river, stream, glacier or wind.

sedimentary rock Rock formed by the squashing and/or heating of layers of sediment.

seed Contains an embryo that can grow into a plant.

selective breeding When organisms are bred to have certain characteristics.

selective herbicide Chemical that only kills certain types of plants.

semen Mixture of sperm cells and fluids.

series Circuit where electrical components are connected one after the other along one wire.

sex cell Cell used to create a new organism.

sexual reproduction Reproduction that needs a male sex cell and a female sex cell.

slide A piece of glass on which a specimen is put.

small intestine Organ that make enzymes to digest foods and absorbs digested food.

solar cell Converts light energy into electrical energy.

solar eclipse When the Moon blocks light from the Sun reaching the Earth.

solar panel Panel containing tubes of water that heat up from the Sun.

Solar System The Sun, planets, moons and asteroids.

solid Solids don't flow, keep their shapes, keep their volumes, cannot be squashed.

solubility How much solute can dissolve in a certain amount of a liquid.

soluble Something that can dissolve in a liquid.

solute Solid that dissolves in a solvent.

solution Solute dissolved in a solvent.

solvent Liquid part of a solution. Will dissolve a solute.

sound energy Energy that carries sounds.

sound wave Areas of squashed and unsquashed particles moving through a material.

soundproofing Using materials that don't allow sound through them easily to make buildings quieter.

south pole Pole of a magnet that points South if the magnet is allowed to turn freely.

South pole The bottom of the Southern hemisphere.

Southern hemisphere Half the Earth below the equator.

space probe Machine sent into space to explore.

species Group of organisms that can breed together to produce offspring that can also reproduce.

specimen Object that you look at using a microscope.

spectrum Range of colours produced when white light is split.

speed Distance travelled in a certain time.

speed–time graph Graph showing how speed changes with time.

sperm cell Male sex cell in animals.

sperm duct Tube carrying sperm cells out of the testes.

spore Tiny cell that can grow into a new organism.

stage Area where a slide is placed on a microscope.

stamen The male sexual organ in flowering plants.

star Gigantic ball of fire in space.

starch Type of carbohydrate. The body's main source of energy. It is made by linking glucose molecules linked together. Plants use it as a storage material.

states of matter The three different forms that materials can be in – solid, liquid or gas.

static electricity Force that attracts things with electrical charges towards each other.

stem Plant organ that supports a plant and carries water.

stigma Female part of a flower that receives pollen.

stimulant Drug that increases the activity of nerves.

stoma Hole in a leaf through which gases diffuse. Plural = stomata.

stomach Organ where proteins are digested.

stopping distance The distance a car travels from when a driver sees the need to stop until the car actually stops.

strain energy Energy stored in something that can spring back to its original shape.

strain force Force in thing that is stretched or squashed.

streamlined Smooth shape that reduces drag.

style Female flower part down which a pollen tube grows.

sugars Types of carbohydrates.

sulfur dioxide Compound of sulfur and oxygen. Dissolves in water to form sulfuric acid.

sulfur precipitator Component fitted to factory and power station chimneys to remove sulfur dioxide from the smoke.

Sun Our nearest star.

surface area Total area that the surface of something has.

suspension Tiny insoluble pieces floating in a liquid.

switch Component that makes or closes a gap in a circuit.

symbol Easy-to-draw diagram or code used to represent something. For example, all elements have a one or two letter symbol that is often used instead of the full name of the element.

symbol equation Word equation written out using symbols.

tar Black sticky substance found in cigarette smoke.

tarnish Coating on metals caused by a reaction of the metal with air and/or water.

telescope Device used to magnify distant objects.

temperature How hot or cold something is. Measured in degrees Celsius (°C).

tendon Tissue that links a muscle to a bone.

testis Organ that makes sperm cells. Plural = testes.

texture The shapes and sizes of grains in a rock and how they fit together.

theory Scientific idea used to explain data.

thermal conductor Material that allows heat energy through it easily.

thermal insulator Material that doesn't allow heat energy through it easily.

thermit reaction Displacement reaction between aluminium and iron oxide:

  aluminium + iron oxide → aluminium oxide + iron

thermometer Device to measure temperatures.

thinking distance The distance a car travels from when a driver thinks about stopping until the brake is pressed.

thorax Middle section of an insect's body.

tissue Lots of the same type of cell grouped together.

top predator Predator at the end of a food chain.

toxic Poisonous.

trachea Windpipe.

transfer When energy is changed or carried from place to place it is transferred.

transform To change.

translucent Translucent substances (like paper) let some light through them but are not see-through.

transmit Allow through.

transparent See-through.

trend Pattern seen in a graph.

tuff Igneous rock formed from volcanic ash.

turbine Has fans or blades that cause it to turn when a liquid or a gas flows into it. A turbine is usually used to turn a generator.

turning effect Another term for 'moment'.

umbilical cord Connects the developing fetus to the placenta, carrying oxygen and all nutrients to the fetus and waste products from the fetus.

unbalanced forces Two forces acting on something that are opposite but are not equal.

universal indicator Liquid or papers that change colour depending on the pH.

Universe Everything in the whole of space.

upthrust A force that a fluid pushes up with.

Uranus Seventh planet from the Sun in the Solar System.

ureter Tube carrying urine into the kidneys.

urethra Tube carrying urine out of a body.

uterus Female organ where an embryo grows.

vaccination Having an injection to stop you getting a disease.

vaccine A weak or dead microbe injected into the body to stimulate the production of antibodies to protect you from the disease.

vacuole 'Bag' inside a plant cell for support and storage.

vacuum 'Nothingness'.

vagina Female organ where the penis is placed during sex.

variable Another name for a 'factor'.

variation The differences between living things.

variety Group of plants of the same species that share similar characteristics.

vein Blood vessel that carries blood towards the heart.

ventilation Movement of air into and out of the lungs.

Venus Second planet from the Sun in the Solar System.

vertebrates Animals that have backbones.

vibrating Moving back and forth.

villus Tiny finger-like structure found in the lining of the small intestine which absorbs digested food. Plural = villi.

virus Smallest type of microbe.

vitamin Nutrient in food that you need tiny amounts of to stay healthy – e.g. vitamin C is used to help cells stick together properly.

volt (V) The unit for voltage.

voltage The difference in electrical energy between two points. Measured in volts (V). It is a measure of the amount of 'pushing power' that makes a current flow around a circuit.

voltmeter Component used to measure voltages.

volume The amount of space that something takes up.

wasted energy The non-useful energy made by something.

water resistance Friction caused by things moving through water.

waterlogged Completely full of water.

watt (W) Unit for power rating. 1 W = 1 J/s.

wavelength The wavelength of a wave is the distance between two complete waves.

weathering Being worn away.

weed Plant that is not wanted.

weedkiller Chemical that kills plants. Also called a herbicide.

weight The force of the Earth's gravity on something.

white blood cell Blood cell that helps destroy microbes.

word equation Diagram showing the reactants in a chemical reaction followed by an arrow pointing to the products.

xylem tube Tube that carries water in plants.

year The length of time a planet takes to orbit the Sun.

yield Amount of useful material that is obtained from a crop.